Nepal
New Horizons?

Contents

Introduction   3
The land and the people   4
History of a kingdom   6
An agricultural economy   10
On foot in the hills   17
A land of many gods   20
Women in Nepali society   26
Health in the hills   33
Education   37
Nepal's working children   39
Giant neighbours   42
Flight from Bhutan   44
Tourism: who benefits?   47
Whose environmental problem?   53
People power   60
Facts and figures   62
Oxfam in Nepal   63
Further reading   64

Acknowledgements
Thanks to the many people whose experiences have enriched this book: the Oxfam Nepal team, who helped me to interpret my research; Tim Malyon, whose photographs are only the visible part of his much greater contribution; Ro Cole, who gave the book its themes, and helped to update it. Thanks also to Michael Hutt who read an early draft; Gopal Chitrakar for the use of the photo on p.8; and the Gurkha Museum for the photo on p.19.

Cover photo Jeremy Hartley/Oxfam

Designed by Oxfam Design Department
Printed and published by Oxfam (UK and Ireland)
274 Banbury Road, Oxford OX2 7DZ, UK
ISBN 0 85598 290 X
© Oxfam (UK and Ireland) 1996
Oxfam UK and Ireland is a member of Oxfam International and is a registered charity, no. 202918

Tim Malyon/Oxfam

Omar Sattaur

Crispin Zeeman

Peter McCulloch/Oxfam

Annemarie Papatheofilou

Peter McCulloch/Oxfam

Nepal presents different faces to the visitor, from the bustling narrow streets of the capital, Kathmandu (above), to the isolation and silence of the high mountains (below). Religion is very much a part of everyday life. Passers by turn Buddhist prayer wheels at the roadside in Kathmandu (top left). Prayer flags flutter above a Buddhist shrine (far left). Head of a lion, the fierce guardian of the richly gilded Buddhist monastery of Kwa Bahal in Patan (left).

Tim Malyon/Oxfam

Introduction

The picture-postcard image of Nepal in the West is of a remote paradise where high mountains protect an ancient culture from contamination by the modern world. The dream-like quality of this image was enhanced a generation ago when Kathmandu became a popular stopping-off place for Westerners on a hippie pilgrimage in search of enlightenment or oblivion.

The reality which greets the visitor today is more complex. Kathmandu suffers the problems of any other present-day city, of teeming traffic and choking pollution, although in much of the country, walking is the only means of travel. Temples and wayside shrines are everywhere, and religious observance an integral part of everyday life. Yet mass tourism is having profound effects on Nepali life, effects which are not always beneficial. Western values are beginning to affect many traditional aspects of life in Nepal. According to one commentator: 'Twenty-five years ago, you would be offered *chhang* [rice beer] in any of the houses in this village. Now, when the wedding season comes, villagers compete to see who can provide the most bottles of *San Miguel*.' However, away from the tourist trails, rural life has changed little over the centuries. Although the Westerner visiting Kathmandu will find it possible to buy most of what he or she would regard as the necessities of civilised life, many Nepalis cannot even afford enough food to keep healthy. For Nepal is one of the poorest countries in the world.

In the early months of 1990, Nepal was in the news for a reason other than the latest ascent of Everest. On our TV screens and newspapers were pictures of violent police suppression of public demonstrations against the government. The first demonstrations took place on 18 February. Just seven weeks later, on 9 April, people took to the streets again, this time to celebrate the success of the pro-democracy movement. The people of Kathmandu Valley had forced King Birendra Bir Bikram Shah Dev to relinquish his political power and become a constitutional monarch, and had reasserted their right to participate in the running of their country. No longer could Nepal be seen as a peaceful, semi-feudal Shangri-La.

Cutting fodder near Putak village, in the mountains. Rural life in Nepal has changed little over the centuries.

Tim Malyon/Oxfam

The land and the people

Tim Malyon/Oxfam

The landscape of Nepal is among the most diverse in the world, ranging from tundra in the high Himalaya to tropical forest in the terai. This diversity is echoed in the rich variety of the people: there are at least 70 different ethnic groups living in Nepal, each with their own distinct history, costume, and culture, and 30 different languages are spoken. For most, there is little contact with the outside world and the isolation of the mountain valleys have further helped to conserve cultural differences.

Climate and soils vary considerably, determining how people use the land, and how many can live in a given area. North-south rivers have cut deep gorges through the mountains, dividing them into more than 25 distinct ranges. These rivers endow the country with ample water, not only for drinking and irrigation, but for generating hydropower. However, very little of the country's hydropower potential has so far been exploited.

The Himalaya are not only the world's highest mountain ranges but some of the most geologically active, continuing to grow at a rate of 1 to 4 millimetres per year and producing frequent earthquakes and landslides. The high mountains are populated by people of broadly Tibetan origin. Farmers divert water from the ice-blue mountain streams into channels which irrigate small patches of land on the valley floors. There they grow barley, wheat, maize, potatoes, beans and buckwheat. On the high and virtually barren mountainsides, sheep and yak cover enormous ground in search of pasture. Unirrigated land in the high mountainous areas cannot support food crops. The limited supply of irrigable land, poor grazing, and harsh climate is reflected in the low population density of 25 people per square kilometre. The Tibetan-speaking Nepalese who live there, and other groups such as the Manangi and Dolpa, make up just under 9 per cent of the total population. They have developed cultural traditions of interdependency and mutual support that enable

them to exist in this bleak environment.

Moving southward, conifer forest and lusher pasture, where people graze cows and buffalo, clothe the corrugation of hills where about 48 per cent of Nepalese live. The land is more fertile than in the mountains but just as prone to landslides. This is where other Tibetan and Tibeto-Burman ethnic groups such as Gurung, Magar, Rai, Limbu, Sherpa, and Tamang live, as well as some Newars. There, too, live the caste groups of Aryan or Indo-European origin, the high-status Brahmin and Chhetri and the low-status occupational castes.

In this part of Nepal, even the poorest tend to own homesteads and have small landholdings. Rice, maize and millet are the staple crops, supported by vegetables and forest products including ferns and fruit. Inheritance law is such that a father's land is divided up amongst his sons, leading to smaller and smaller parcels of land being farmed. Land is in such short supply that people are being driven to terrace extremely steep hillsides or to over-graze and over-exploit forest land. Most of the land is rain-fed and loss of soil on degraded and overexploited land has been as high as 200 tonnes per hectare per year during monsoon months. These pressures, and the lack of alternative sources of income, are making livelihoods in the middle hills increasingly unsustainable, and lead to seasonal and permanent migration from the hills.

Most of the potentially irrigable 2 million hectares of arable land lies in the terai, Nepal's main food-producing area. The land is made fertile by the silt washed down by the rivers, and the climate favours three crops per year. Population density is much higher, 193 per square km, reflecting not only the more favourable conditions for agriculture but also the greater opportunities for work in the fledgling industries that are springing up in the terai. Some 44 per cent of the population live here, including Brahmin, Chhetri, Tharu, occupational castes and indigenous peoples, but land distribution is much less equitable than it is in the hills. Land-holdings are larger and land-owners depend much more on casual labourers, supplied by immigrants from the hills and landless from the terai.

Opposite page: Jhong Kola valley, above Kagbeni. Communities living in the high mountain valleys have developed independently of each other, preserving their individual cultures, languages, and ways of life.

Left: Hindu girl in her ceremonial finery.

Below: Buddhist monk passing a wayside shrine, near Upper Mustang.

Tim Malyon/Oxfam

History of a kingdom

Prithvi Narayan Shah became ruler of Gorkha, a small kingdom of Western Nepal, in 1742 at the age of 22. His ambition to gain for Gorkha some of the fabled wealth of the kingdoms of the Kathmandu Valley, and his vision of a nation united against the encroaching British East India Company, led him to begin the military campaigns that transformed Nepal into a single kingdom. The once-separate kingdoms of the Kathmandu Valley, Kathmandu, Patan and Bhaktapur, fell to Prithvi Narayan in 1768 and 1769 and, within five years, most of Eastern Nepal was also his.

The Shah monarchy remained in power until 1846 when, following a massacre in which 32 of Nepal's leading nobles were slaughtered, Jang Bahadur Rana assumed control of the country as the first of a line of hereditary Rana Prime Ministers that ruled Nepal for more than a century. During this period, the monarchy exercised little power and the Ranas assured its cooperation and their security by marrying into the royal family.

Rana rule brought little improvement in the lives of the common citizens. The treasury was regarded as Rana family property and Nepal was closed to the rest of the world, although Jang Bahadur, who visited Britain and France, and his successors were intoxicated with things European. To this day Kathmandu is littered with neo-Classical palaces and buildings that seem strikingly out of place in a country that has never been colonised.

For rural Nepalis, life had changed very little from medieval times. They had no relationship with the rulers save through tax officials who would impose taxes, administer law, and exact unpaid labour as they saw fit.

Political change was initiated by expatriate Nepalis based in India. In 1947, influenced by Indian politics, they formed what was to become the Nepali Congress. Their aim was to replace the Rana government with a democratic government under King Tribhuvan. The King fled to Delhi. Indian Prime Minister Nehru brokered an agreement between the King, the Nepali Congress, and Prime Minister Mohun Shamsher Rana. The King returned to Nepal in 1951 and installed an interim cabinet, which failed within a few months, and Mohun Shamsher, the last of the Ranas, had no option but to resign.

After the death of King Tribhuvan in 1955 his son, Mahendra, ascended the throne. King Mahendra's rule marked the beginning of Nepal's modern period. He reestablished contact with China and forged diplomatic links with the USA and France. He brought Nepal into the UN fold and initiated a flow of aid into the country that has increased ever since. Nepal began to change as foreigners and alien ideas began to permeate society.

Experiment in democracy

On 12 February 1959, King Mahendra proclaimed a new democratic constitution and announced that elections were to be held. The Nepali Congress had the overwhelming majority and Bisheswor Prasad Koirala became Nepal's first elected Prime Minister. He lost no time in introducing radical reforms, the most controversial of which was a land reform act that abolished *birta* land-ownership (*birtas* were lands granted to individuals for past services rendered to the state). The act struck at the elite and disrupted the status quo. Maintaining law and order became an increasing problem for the new government.

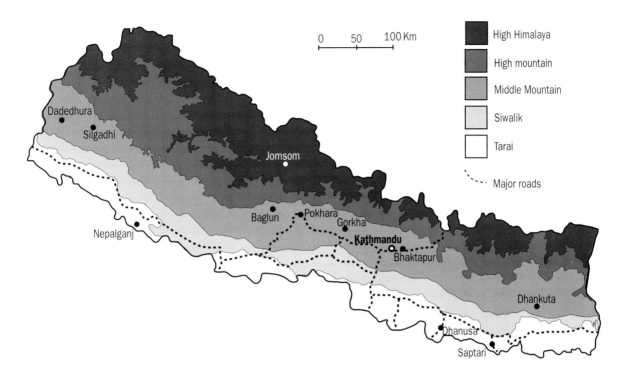

A minor rebellion in Gorkha gave the King a reason to invoke emergency powers, disband the Koirala government and reassume power, after just 19 months of democratic government. King Mahendra blamed the Koirala government for failing to fulfil its 'democratic duties' and imprisoned Cabinet members. He declared that the Nepali people were not yet ready for Western-style democracy and, with his advisors, designed a unique system of government that came to be known as Party-less Panchayat Democracy.

Panchayat means village council; the system's aim being to represent the voice of villagers. The adult population of each village would elect an 11-person Village Panchayat. Each of these would send a representative to the District Assembly which would then elect an 11-member District Panchayat. Members of all District Panchayats of one Zone formed a Zonal Assembly from which a Zonal Committee was nominated. The Rastriya Panchayat, or national parliament, had 125 seats and was made up of members of each district, elected from the Zonal Assemblies. The King selected the holders of 20 per cent of the seats in the Rastriya Panchayat. He was at the centre of power, supported by his chosen Council of Ministers.

The system was supposed to diffuse the power of the elites and avoid ethnic tension. But the old ways of patronage and favour linked to caste and status persisted, and a new and stronger elite was created. The lack of political parties served only to focus more attention on religious and ethnic divisions; and village voices had no better chance of being heard than before.

King Mahendra died in 1972 and was followed by the present King, Birendra, from whom the people expected great changes. Educated at St. Joseph's College in Darjeeling, Eton, and the Universities of Tokyo and Harvard, the King was reputed to be liberal and concerned about Nepal's development.

A huge student demonstration on 6 April 1979, to mourn the death of Zulfikar Ali Bhutto in Pakistan, was violently crushed by police, sparking off strikes and protests throughout the country. Demonstrators marched on the Royal

Palace in Kathmandu on 23 May, setting fire to several government buildings. King Birendra's response was to speak on Radio Nepal to announce a national referendum in which people could choose a reformed Panchayat system or the reintroduction of multiparty democracy.

Suddenly, the ban on political parties that had been enforced since 1961 was lifted and, for one year leading up to the referendum, all parties were allowed to campaign. Restrictions on publishing were set aside, censorship ceased and political reporting flourished. On 2 May 1980, the people voted by a slim majority to retain the Panchayat system, but with reforms.

The passing of autocratic rule

The reforms included amending the Constitution to allow direct election of the members of the Rastriya Panchayat for the first time. The Rastriya Panchayat would then elect the Cabinet. The next three years were characterised by an increasingly unstable government, racked by revelations of high level scandals implicating not only ministers but members of the royal family. Banned political parties capitalised on the publicity and intensified their agitation. Police repression likewise intensified. Rishikesh Shah, a former minister, founded the Human Rights Organisation of Nepal in response to the government's increasing repression.

India's decision not to renew a trade and transit treaty with Nepal added to the government's difficulties. Piqued by Nepal's purchase of arms from China and its granting of business contracts to Chinese firms, India closed off all but two of its border posts and hindered the passage of Nepali imports from third countries. There were shortages of essential supplies, and widespread hardship and discontent. Opposition parties began to capitalise on the growing unrest.

As those in urban areas followed on television the enormous changes sweeping Eastern Europe in the autumn of 1989, and as the Panchayat government struggled to maintain power, people everywhere prepared for a change they knew would have to come. The King's failure to announce any political reforms at a government rally in Pokhara, in Western Nepal, appeared to be the last straw. Mass demonstrations and general strikes brought the country to a standstill. The King at last responded by announcing a new Cabinet which was to begin talks with the banned parties, investigate the killings that had occurred

Supporters of democracy clash with pro-Panchayat workers during the first day of agitation in the capital.

during the unrest, and establish a commission to amend the constitution. An estimated half a million people from Kathmandu and Patan took to the streets.

The demonstrators gathered on the parade ground in central Kathmandu. Everything appeared peaceful, the police watchful but tolerant, until people began to move towards the Palace, shouting anti-Royalty slogans. Suddenly, soldiers appeared and opened fire with machine guns. Demonstrations followed all over the Valley and clashes with police resulted in more deaths. On 8 April, the King lifted the ban on political parties and, on 15 April 1990 announced the formation of an interim government under the leadership of Congress veteran Krishna Prasad Bhattarai.

Democracy at village level

Nepal's is an intensely hierarchical society, where status and power are largely based on caste and ethnicity. The country was isolated from outside influences for centuries; most of its people knew only of the feudal relationship between lords and serfs and their place in society as determined by their caste. The forms of government were modelled on Hindu concepts of a divine ruler; the King has traditionally been believed to be an incarnation of the god Vishnu, there to protect the people, dispense justice, and punish wrongdoers. These social relationships, geographical isolation, and the lack of a common enemy to fight against, such as Indians found in the British colonisers, may explain the almost total lack of political organisation at grassroots level until the 1940s.

The popular movement that led to the restoration of democracy in Nepal represents a sea-change in the way that ordinary people in Nepal view their government and in the demands they make of it. The success of the movement has imbued the nation with a new-found confidence. The opportunities for participating in government have never been greater. As well as voting for a parliamentary candidate of the party of their choice, people also enjoy increasing opportunities to participate in local government. The governments so far elected have aimed to increase the resources such as water, electricity, schooling, health care and so on, for ordinary citizens. The management of all of these services is by local government officials who are elected locally. All sections of civil society, including non-governmental organisations (NGOs) have recognised that the scene is set for greater participation and are making increasing use of their new opportunities and freedom.

Economic and political uncertainty

Unrealistic promises by the formerly banned political parties raised high expectations among a population that was impatient to taste the fruits of 'development'. There was little appreciation of the time it would take the Nepali Congress government to sort out which policies among those it inherited were worth keeping and what should be rejected.

The Nepali Congress Government, while espousing the cause of democratic socialism, in the same breath preached the virtue of privatising government-owned industries, tightening belts, curbing government expenditure, and abolishing subsidies, and expounded the benefits of economic liberalisation: stimulating industrial growth, encouraging exports, and pulling the crutches away from limping, inefficient industries. This programme had only been in place for three years when the Congress government collapsed and was replaced by a minority Communist government in November 1994, which, faced by the realities of globalisation of the world economy and Nepal's place in it, differed in economic policy only in emphasis. In this knowledge, the Communist government instead tried to pay greater attention to a political programme. At the time of writing the minority government has fallen, to be replaced by a coalition dominated by the Nepali Congress. Once again the future is uncertain.

An agricultural economy

Nepal is one of the world's poorest countries. Average incomes are barely above survival level, and half of all children under five are malnourished. Nepal's economy is based on agriculture. But poor soils, difficult terrain, uncertain climate, and skewed land distribution mean that Nepal has continuously been unable to produce sufficient food to meet the needs of its people. The government has tried to tackle this by increasing irrigation, subsidising agricultural inputs, and providing credit. Of the total 2 million hectares of agricultural land deemed potentially irrigable, 1.3 million is in the terai and the remainder in the hills and mountains. To date, about 943,000 ha has been irrigated, of which 743,000 ha is in the terai. Government statistics show that productivity from irrigation schemes managed by groups of farmers have been far higher than from those managed by government.

Nepali farmers are probably among the best in the world. Consider that the average paddy yield per hectare of arable land for 1955 to 1960 was 4.56 tonnes for Japan and 2.54 tonnes for China. In the best-managed farmland in the Kathmandu Valley, it is 4.3 tonnes. Witness the vast and steep mountainsides north of the Mahabharat range, converted into neat terraces that have been

In the foothills of the Himalaya, near Kathmandu. Terracing enables crops to be grown on steep hillsides. Because of the shortage of land in the middle hills, even the steepest hillsides are cultivated.

Jeremy Hartley/Oxfam

Carrying fodder cut from communal fields, Putak village.

shaped to extract the maximum arable area from the topography, and the skill of the farmers is immediately apparent. They divert water to protect terraces threatened by collapse, they fertilise poor fields with top soil from nutrient-rich areas and they work constantly to keep terraces in good condition.

Increases in cropping intensity, irrigation, fertiliser use, mechanisation, and the availability of improved varieties of food crops and livestock have led to higher productivity per unit area, but a simultaneous growth in population has not only consumed that increase but caused a nett food deficit. Major land

Spinning wool with a drop spindle, Kalopani village.

Making a basket used for transporting a wide variety of goods.

reform would appear to be the only way of satisfying the food requirements of rural farming families.

The manufacturing sector is very small, contributing only 9 per cent of GDP, handicapped by a lack of infrastructure, skills, and capital, and by competition from India. Nepal is very dependent on its huge southern neighbour for markets and export routes. The most profitable exports are carpets and garments. Most manufacturing firms are very small, with only a few employees, or run as cottage industries.

Nepal has to look to external sources for investment capital. In 1987 the government obtained a loan from the International Monetary Fund, on condition that it implemented a programme of structural adjustment, reducing government expenditure and privatising state-owned enterprises. Nepal also receives substantial amounts of development aid.

Living off the land

The majority of Nepali families live in their own houses and farm their own lands; 90 per cent of adults are farmers, or work in jobs related to agriculture. Walking through the mountain and hill villages, visitors are struck by the beauty and peacefulness of the landscape. For many, there is a thrill of discovering an older way of life. The further one walks, the greater the sense of isolation from the modern world. People make what they need from local materials. Even in terai villages, much better serviced by roads and telecommunications, one is struck by the degree of self-sufficiency of most households. At first glance, then, rural Nepali life appears idyllic.

For most families, however, the reality of rural life, hidden from the casual observer, is increasingly harsh. Landlessness, although less common in Nepal than in other South Asian countries, is increasing; and most Nepali farms are too small to provide enough food for their owners. Only in the terai is there no food deficit. There, larger landholdings are common, and agricultural wage labour, sharecropping, or bonded labour, is much more the norm.

In the hill farms, families are able to grow enough food to last only for four to eight months of the year. To make up the shortfall, people have to earn money. They take jobs as porters or work as labourers on the farms of large landowners. They often move away to work in towns in the terai or to Kathmandu or India. Between 1970 and 1981, there was a nett inflow of 397,000 people to the terai, whereas the mountain regions suffered a nett loss of 192,000 and the hills a loss of 204,000 people. In addition to these permanent migrants, millions migrate on a seasonal basis. Living off the land has become less and less viable.

Population pressure and a severely skewed distribution of agricultural land account for the increasing hardship faced by rural Nepalis. The 'carrying capacity' of the land has been exceeded in large parts of the country. For example, the Far West is only sparsely populated but there is so little agricultural land available, and it is of such low quality, that *pressure* on the land is high. In contrast, there is less pressure in the terai, although far more people live there. Pressure is most acute in the densely populated western hills and mountains.

The attractiveness of life in a remote rural area diminishes when basic needs are not met. For rural Nepalis, it often means a life cut off from a market in which to sell their produce, difficult access to hospitals, schools and colleges, banks and government resources, and social deprivation.

Land reform

Of the country's land area 14.718 million ha, 15 per cent is under permanent ice and snow. Only 2.6 million ha (18 per cent) is cultivable, and the distribution of this land is very skewed. The national average landholding is 0.92 ha, but 60 per cent of landholdings are below the average size. In 1981, the larger landowners with more than 3 ha accounted for 9 per cent of farm households but occupied 48 per cent of the cultivable land. The gap between large and small landholdings is largest in the terai, where 54 per cent of country's cultivable land is to be found. Distribution is more equitable in the mid hills — very few households are landless — but very few have enough land to feed their families.

In 1964, the government attempted to address the problem of land distribution

Farmhouse in the Kathmandu valley. Family plots are small and few people are able to grow sufficient food for a whole year.

Threshing rice. Women and men share some agricultural tasks.

in its Land Reform Act. The Act sought to redistribute land more equitably, provide farmers with technology and resources to boost productivity, and divert unproductive capital and human resources from land to other sectors of the economy. The ceilings for landholdings were set too high, however, to release more than 23,000 ha, less than 1 per cent of the total cultivable land. The Act also provided certain rights to those who had worked the same piece of land for more than one year. Landowners wishing to dispose of tenanted land have to give first priority to tenants who, by virtue of the Act, are entitled to ownership of 25 per cent of the land they cultivate. The Act also entitled tenants to half the gross annual produce of the land they work.

However, the Act is rarely implemented. Of the 1.8 million tenants identified following enactment, only 300,000 received formal certificates of tenancy. An estimated 40 per cent of tenants were omitted from the process. Despite the provisions of the 1964 Land Reform Act, sharecroppers receive, at worst, one third of the crop and, at best, half the crop. The *kamaiya*, bonded agricultural labourers of the Mid and Far West, receive considerably less.

The life of a bonded labourer

Bang Purawa is a quiet hamlet in Nepal's westernmost terai district. The farmhouses and outbuildings are well maintained, with tiled roofs and spacious courtyards. They are surrounded by flat farmland, as far as the eye can see. Away from the farmhouses are smaller, one-storey mud-and-wattle buildings. In such a building lives 46-year-old Ram Bahadur Chaudhury.

Ram Bahadur once lived with his parents, and his aunt and uncle and cousins, in one house. His father and uncle had over many years accumulated a debt of Rs 20,000. When Ram Bahadur's father died, the family decided to split the responsibility for paying off the debt between the sons. So, Ram Bahadur started his independent life with an inherited debt of Rs 5,000.

Over the years, he has had to borrow money from his landlord to pay for extra food, clothing, and incidental expenses at festivals. Ram Bahadur is neither literate nor numerate but remembers that, five years ago, his debt was Rs 14,640. Today, his debt amounts to Rs 35,000. He has kept no records and is at a loss to explain the rapid escalation of the debt.

His present circumstances preclude the possibility of his ever repaying the debt. He has to provide for a further eight family members, none of whom earn. Ram Bahadur works his landlord's fields from dawn to dusk every day, for which he is paid annually 14 quintals of rice, 5 litres of cooking oil, 50 kg of flour and 2.5 kg salt; enough, Ram Bahadur estimates, to last six to seven months. Ram Bahadur's wife has to work in the landlord's household, threshing and winnowing, feeding animals and cleaning their sheds, while his daughter helps the landlord's wife with the household chores. For this his wife and daughter are not paid, but are given one meal a day. Ram Bahadur would like to quit his position, but that means finding a new landlord who will pay off his debt, and that is not probable.

Ram Bahadur's predicament is a common one in Far West Nepal. Strictly speaking, *kamaiya* are annual contract workers; but in effect Ram Bahadur is a bonded labourer, a modern form of slave whose debt keeps him poor, at the beck and call of his master and subject to his master's whims. Slavery and the sale of human beings is illegal in Nepal. But every winter, markets are held in the towns of the Mid and Far West where *kamaiya* can seek new masters and masters seek new *kamaiya* by paying off their debts. Obviously, as in Ram Bahadur's case, the larger the debt the more unlikely it is that a *kamaiya* will be able to find a new master.

Ram Bahadur tending his master's cattle.

Ram Bahadur is a Tharu, one of the indigenous tribes of the terai whose ancestors, by virtue of their tolerance of malaria, were able to live in the dense forests which then covered the plains. Following the malaria eradication campaign of the 1960s, many of the Tharu were dispossessed of their lands by *paharia*, immigrants from the hills encouraged by the Kathmandu government to settle there. Thousands of Tharu became labourers on other people's farms.

The *kamaiya* system is said to be a corruption of a more benign feudal system prevalent among earlier Tharu communities. Even today, *kamaiya* working for Tharu landlords appear to be better treated than those working for *paharia*. *Kamaiya* are exploited because of their inability to read and calculate and their ignorance even of the most basic of human rights. Debts are often falsely inflated and rarely are *kamaiya* given enough to survive on, much less pay off a debt. A survey of 17,728 *kamaiya* found that 98 per cent were landless, 95 per cent illiterate, and 30 per cent were indebted to their masters. Of the latter, fewer than 7 per cent could give any information about their debt. They are expected to work up to 18 hours per day, for payment which is a combination of land, produce, shelter, basic clothing, and cash, and which is always insufficient to meet the needs of the family.

Ram Bahadur is receiving help from an NGO called Backward Society Education (BASE) run by Dilli Chaudhury, himself a Tharu. BASE's strategy is to raise awareness of the infringement of human rights through adult non-formal education classes and to encourage *kamaiya* to save. BASE gives Rs 100 for every Rs 300 saved by the *kamaiya*. When there is enough money to purchase new land, BASE registers it in the *kamaiya*'s wife's name and the family occupy the new land. Dilli Chaudhury's view is that, since sale and trafficking of human beings contradicts Article 20 of the 1990 Constitution, and since the loans are illegal, there is nothing to stop *kamaiya* leaving their landlords.

Jeremy Hartley/Oxfam

Rice fields just before harvest, near Koplang. Rice is one of the staples of the Nepalese diet.

On foot in the hills

In the shade of a pipal and a banyan tree is a stone seat, or *chautara*, where porters can unburden themselves of their loads and rest their legs. This is the nearest Nepal has to the motorway service station, for this is how most people travel; on foot, on small mountain paths. Everything that is needed in the middle hills and mountains, from Coca Cola to concrete, is brought in *dokos*, wicker baskets, on the backs of porters.

The spectacular hills, leading up to the snow peaks that so attract the mountaineer and outdoor tourist, make life extremely arduous for their inhabitants. The Himalayan barrier to the north has led to

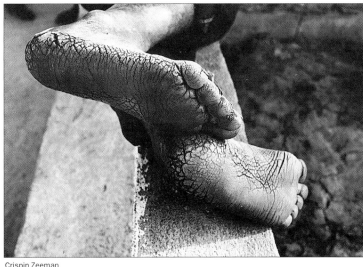

Crispin Zeeman

Indian domination of Nepal's economy; the nearest port is at Calcutta, 1000 km from Kathmandu and reachable only through Indian territory, and air-freight is prohibitively expensive for all but the wealthiest. Even if air freight were widely affordable, most of the 50 or so airstrips in operation would still have to rely on mules or porters to transport the goods to the villages. And of the country's 10,000km of roads, only a third are metalled and almost all are in the terai. Invaluable though they are, these roads serve few of the 44 per cent of the Nepalese who live there. The remainder rely on porters or on their own feet to transport themselves and their goods around. Travelling between two villages only 15km apart may involve an eight-hour walk, which descends 800m before climbing 2,000m. Health care and primary education may be a few hours' walk away and trade even with neighbouring valleys can be severely limited. A *chautara* is always a welcome sight.

Above: Feet of a porter, asleep on a *chautara*.

Left: Porters fording a stream. The only way to reach the isolated settlements in the hills is on foot.

Apples and markets

Marpha a village in lower Mustang, grows some of the most delicious apples in Nepal. Their presence in the area is a result of the activities in Marpha of the National Temperate Horticulture Research Station (NTHRS), set up 27 years ago. Apple-growing was the station's first project and Chhatra Bahadur Thakali was one of the first farmers to see its potential, even though he knew that it meant waiting five years to harvest his first fruit.

But harvesting a crop is only the first step. 'Production is good but there is no market', Chhatra Bahadur explains. The apples, though much tastier than the Indian varieties available in Kathmandu, an hour away by air, are affected by the economic forces that keep farmers in this region comparatively poor.

Some of the apples find their way to Pokhara. Porters bring in tea, sugar and other provisions not available in Mustang from Pokhara, and return loaded with apples. But even this has its problems, said Chhatra Bahadur. 'I tried transporting apples by mule to Pokhara. But the drivers don't take care. A third of my apples would be damaged during transit.' Storing the apples helps a little; six months after harvest, the price rises; but then, after six months there are ten apples to the kilogram compared to six when they are freshly harvested.

The station has trained farmers in drying apples and making apple brandy and cider. Over the years it has introduced cauliflower, broccoli, red radish, onion, garlic, improved varieties of potato, carrots, cabbage as well as improved varieties of indigenous fruits and vegetables which all thrive. Although such products may fetch better prices than fresh apples, growers face the same problems of a remote market and costly freight charges. For apples, it means that about a quarter of Mustang's total annual harvest of 1,500 tonnes rots; not surprisingly farmers are no longer interested in establishing apple orchards.

A road, however, might change their minds. 'Most farmers, if a motorable road comes, would be happy to grow apples because it is potentially three to four times more profitable than buckwheat or corn. They'd like a road because they'd be able to reach the market quickly and sell vegetables that are off season in the low lands,' says Chhatra Bahadur.

However, Buddhi Ratna Sherchan, acting chief of the station, disagrees. 'We don't want a road because it brings all sorts of problems, including air pollution and dependency on the outside for oil, plastics and many other things. A ropeway would be better.'

Buddhi Ratna Sherchan, head of the horticulture research station.

Farmers and soldiers: the Gurkha tradition

One way of earning a living for a young man from a poor farming family is to join the British or Indian army as a professional soldier. The link between Britain and Gurkha soldiers stretches back to the early nineteenth century, when the soldiers were recruited to the Imperial Indian Army from across the border. The first three Gurkha regiments were formed in 1815, and Gurkhas have since fought in wars all over the world, including the first and second World Wars. In World War 2, there were 160,000 Gurkha soldiers in the British Army. This number was reduced to 15,000 after the war, and then further reduced between 1969 and 1971, and is to be cut to 2,500 by 1998. However, the Indian army still employs many thousands of Gurkha soldiers.

The tradition is particularly strong in some mountain villages, where it is every young man's ambition to be chosen for the regiments, as the advantages that follow are numerous. Families without a son in the British or Indian Gurkha army are pitied.

Soldiers made redundant from the British army are all granted pensions according to rank and years of service, and are given a six-week resettlement training course which includes such skills as car mechanics, driving, carpentry, masonry, and electrical appliance repair. Over the past decade, the trend has been for returning servicemen to settle in the terai towns on returning to Nepal. They represent the middle class and seek education for their children, fertile agricultural land to invest in, and consumer goods, rather than a return to village life. Others seek work abroad as security guards or drivers, or take up a new career by joining merchant fleets.

Left: Picking apples in Marpha. Growers in this area have a problem in reaching markets for their produce.

Below: A Gurkha Boy Soldier in the 8th Gurkha Rifles circa 1939

Harry Sneldon/ The Gurkha Museum

A land of many gods

A boulder not quite buried by a modern tarmac road is every morning offered fresh flowers and coloured powders; the trees surrounding a monastery are festooned with prayer flags; a Shiva-lingam hewn from stone finds itself in the middle of a raised grass roundabout; an exquisitely cast bronze statue of the winged Garuda kneels in obeisance outside a temple dedicated to Vishnu; a huge bas-relief of Bhairab, carved from stone and painted in vivid colours, dominates the square outside the old royal palace in Kathmandu; deities take many forms in Nepali eyes and forms of worship are just as varied.

Nepali citizens are free to follow any religion they wish to, although it is an offence to proselytise. Buddhism, Tantrism, Islam, and Christianity are all practised in Nepal, as well as the Hindu cults of Shaivism and Vaisnavism. Local religious shamanistic practices have been

Top: One of the two giant Malla wrestlers which flank the stone stairway to the Hindu Nyatapola Temple in Bhaktapur.

Right: Monk studying the Buddhist scriptures.

The inhabitants of the Kathmandu valley who, by the 15th Century came to be known as Newar, absorbed religious ideas from many different sources and their practice and religious art remains distinctive. The carvings on the walls of a fountain in the courtyard of the 17th-Century Patan Durbar show the religious syncretism that is so common in the Kathmandu Valley. Mahalaxmi, Hindu goddess of wealth, beauty and intelligence, seen by tantric Buddhists as Smasaaneswori, Goddess of cremation grounds. She sits above an chain of interlocking Hindu Shiva-linga and Buddhist stupas.

practising Buddhism — Manangi, Thakali, Mustangi, Sherpa, Lepcha, part of the Tamang, Gurung and Newar populations and the people of Humla and Dolpo — would suggest a rather larger population of Buddhists than would the official figure of 8 per cent (approximately 1.5 million).

The borders between religions are not as distinct as one might expect. This is especially true of the Kathmandu valley where the 'ethnic group' now known as Newar (the descendants of migrant ethnic groups from many different parts of Nepal and possibly beyond) employ both Hindu and Buddhist religious leaders to officiate at some of their many festivals and ceremonies. Deities and temples are used by Hindus and Buddhists on different occasions and the same temple may display statues of deities and motifs from both religions.

Left: Hand-held prayer wheel

Below: Statue of the Buddha, Kathmandu.

Peter McCulloch/Oxfam

adapted to incorporate some forms of Hindu or Buddhist worship in many parts of the country, resulting in a wide range of different practices.

Censuses tend not to make distinctions between these different variations, and most are categorised as Hindu or Buddhist. Moreover, for many Hindus, Buddhism is a branch of their religion (although Buddhists would disagree with such a view). The number of ethnic groups

Caste and culture

According to the Nepali anthropologist, Dor Bahadur Bista, the introduction of orthodox Brahminic caste concepts is of comparatively recent origin and more or less confined to the Kathmandu valley. Hinduism had long been practised in Nepal, but the particular Indian brand of hierarchical Hinduism was introduced by more fundamentalist Brahmins fleeing persecution during the Muslim invasion of North India. A concern for self-preservation, rather than any religious mission, writes Bista, characterised these immigrants, who were to have a profound effect on Nepali culture. Hindu caste concepts affect social relationships in many different ways, some of which may be ultimately unimportant, but others greatly influence the course of a person's life.

Caste ideas, in terms of ascribing social status, have touched even non-Hindu ethnic groups. The caste system was legalised in 1854 and outlawed in 1963. The hierarchy of Hindu castes and ethnicities changes according to the ethnic and religious mix of the particular area, but most ethnic groups or castes place themselves somewhere between the two extremes of Brahmin or Chhetri at the top and untouchables at the bottom. Caste ideas have somehow affected even the Nepali Muslims, so that members of one group of Muslims, perceived as lower caste, are considered unsuitable marriage partners for members of a higher caste; an idea totally alien to orthodox Islam.

Language, tone of voice, and manner of speaking changes according to the perceived status of the speakers. Although this may have no import to people who have grown up knowing no other form of social interaction, caste and status matter when they limit a low-caste person's expectations of life, or the benefits such as education or health services they receive from government schemes or foreign aid projects. Caste certainly seems to be important in politics regardless of party: in the general election of 1991, of the 204 Congress candidates, 37 per cent were

Brahmins, as were 47 per cent of the 177 candidates fielded by the Communist Party of Nepal-United Marxist Leninists.

Caste ideas are very strong in the eastern terai or the Far West, for example, where it was until recently considered polluting to a Brahmin to have walked in the shadow cast by an untouchable. Among the newly educated, and in the towns and the Kathmandu valley, caste is breaking down and economic class becoming a much more important divider. Many Brahmins, for example, would not now worry about whether the food they ate in the restaurants of Kathmandu was cooked by another Brahmin.

Dor Bahadur Bista warns against the negative way in which hierarchical caste ideas affect Nepali society and its potential advancement: 'Poor self image, hierarchic caste status and constant defensiveness ... hamper national development through inactivity and conservative reaction.' In what he calls the 'fatalistic culture', society rewards a person for being born of the right family rather than for his or her achievements. Other Nepali intellectuals, while agreeing that Nepali society would be better if it were more egalitarian, believe it is too simplistic to blame a fatalistic culture for Nepal's lack of development.

Houses and social structures

The stone houses and the narrow, paved, main street of the town of Marpha nestle at the foot of the barren hills. Originally built higher up the valley side, Marpha later shifted down to follow a low ridge at the foot of the hills, and has a linear lay out, suiting a town on an important trade route that once linked India, Nepal, and Tibet. But the old site, on less fertile and higher land, and the new both maximise the amount of good land on the valley floor that can be given over to agriculture.

The houses in Marpha are built of rubble bonded together with mud mortar into thick walls. Stables on the ground floor raise the temperature on the upper floors, where the families live. Inner courtyards trap heat and provide a haven from the strong winds that howl up the valley in the late morning. There is hardly any rain in the area, making pitch roofing unnecessary and cheaper, flat roofs the norm. The wood stacked on the front of the roof is not only a show of wealth but protects the mud mortar from erosion by snow melt.

The predominantly Gurung village of Lwang, north of Pokhara, is also built on the higher slopes of the valley, in order to make use of the best land for agriculture. However, in this village, the way the houses are laid out tells something of the

Opposite page, top: The ancient Buddhist stupa of Swayambhunath, is over 2,500 years old.

Opposite page, bottom: Tukche monastery, near Marpha.

Elaborately carved entrance to the ancient courtyard of the Kumari Bahal, a Buddhist monastery where the Kumari, or living goddess, is always in residence.

Annemarie Papatheofilou/Oxfam

23

Right: Ex-Gurkha, making a basket in the courtyard of his house.

status of their occupants; an alien concept to the Buddhists of Marpha and further north. In Lwang, as in many villages in the middle hills, the lower castes build their houses on the perimeter, and the core of the village is reserved for the so-called 'purer', higher castes.

Despite the fact that the Gurungs of Lwang are Tibeto-Burmans who practice Buddhism, caste sentiments still apply. They, along with all other ethnic groups of Nepal, have been allotted a place in the caste hierarchy. Because Gurungs predominate and are considered to be of much higher caste than the occupational castes, their houses are in the centre of the village. Most of the Gurung houses have slate roofs and are well maintained, reflecting the higher incomes of their owners. Corn and hay is stacked high above the ground to keep it safe from animals. Livestock have their own shelter and the first floor of the house may be given over to storage of grain and valuable objects. Many of the houses of the occupational castes of Lwang have thatched roofs and are in a worse state of repair.

The Brahminic concept of purity also extends to food, physical objects, structures, and space. Brahmin houses, for example, have two kitchens. Only the initiated of the family and the heads of the household are allowed to enter the ritual kitchen. This conferring of 'purity' to household spaces is not confined to

The village of Lwang, where houses are arranged according to caste, with lower castes building their houses on the outskirts of the village.

Brahmin homes. In the photograph on the opposite page, a Gurung ex-Gurkha has retired and resumed the life of a farmer. He sits in the open courtyard of his house, making a *doko*, a traditional basket used by porters. The courtyard is also a play area for children, a place to sit and gossip, to dry and thresh grain, and to receive visitors; the milder climate of the middle hills makes for a more outdoor life. A lower-caste villager may be admitted to the courtyard but not to the verandah, which is reserved for friends or higher-caste visitors. Rooms inside the house are also similarly differentiated.

Right: Intricate woodcarving is a feature of traditional building style in Nepal.

Below: The courtyard is the setting for many activities: children play there, food is prepared, and visitors entertained.

Women in Nepali society

Generalisations about any country are always subject to qualification and this is even more so in the case of Nepal, with its great diversity of ethnicities and lifestyles. The fact that Nepali society values women less than men, however, seems to hold true for virtually all caste and ethnic groups. From the Himalaya to the terai, women have lower status and heavier workloads than do men.

Many parents treat boys preferentially from birth, and this inequality in treatment continues through life. Girls, particularly in the more orthodox Hindu communities of the terai, are fed less, educated less, and deprived of opportunities for self-development. This bias is reflected in population statistics, for all three geographical regions. According to the 1981 census, boys outnumbered girls in the 0-14 years age group by 240,000. The same trend is true for all age groups and is believed to result from unequal access to resources throughout life. Nepal is one of the few countries of the world where women have a lower life expectancy than men.

A Hindu girl learns to view her membership of the family she is born into as temporary, since she must eventually leave it for her husband's household. She learns to accept that the best food, care, and attention will go to her brothers. In Hindu society, she ideally grows up to be submissive and obedient. The only status she derives in society is in relation to her father, husband, and sons.

Sons have always inherited most of the assets when the parent dies. If the parents are rich, the daughter inherits some of the property, but rarely land. In August 1995, the Supreme Court ruled that the govern-

ment has one year in which to bring legislation on inheritance which treats men and women equally. It is likely to be some years before the impact of that ruling is felt, since it is not common practice to settle family matters by resorting to law. Nonetheless, it is an outcome of the changed socio-political environment created by the new democracy which will eventually play its part in enhancing the status of women.

The amount of power women have, though always less than that of men, varies according to caste and ethnic group. Among the Hindu castes and some Tibeto-Burman hill communities, for example, women are less able than men to move from the predominant subsistence economy into cash employment. In contrast, women of the Tibetan-speaking mountain communities have more power over decisions affecting the household and may sometimes even handle the household finances.

Above: Weaving cloth for use by the household, on a traditional back-strap loom, Ulleri village.

Left: Buddhist nun, reading sacred texts at a nunnery near Muktinath.

Opposite page: Resting on the way to the fields. Night soil is carried from the village in baskets, for use as manure to enrich the soil.

Digging carrots. These women are taking part in a community development project set up to encourage the growing of vegetables.

In the rice-planting season, the day begins at 3.00am for Damber Kumari. In other seasons, she rises at 5.00am. She makes the fire, heats the water and makes the buffalo food from the previous day's leftovers. The house must be swept and the floor re-covered with a thin paste of red clay. Damber Kumari then fills the brass pots with water, lights the incense, and prays with her husband. They have tea at 7.00am after which Damber Kumari makes corn bread and *dal-bhat*, the staple food of lentil and rice, or *dido*, a cooked dough of ground millet or corn. She makes enough to eat now, and for a second meal later in the day.

By 9.00am she and her husband will go to the fields. If there is no pressing work to do there, she may collect fodder, or weave, or spin wool. At 3.00pm she will eat again. She usually returns home around 7.00pm, cooks, eats, and retires to sleep.

Lwang women sow the major crops, cultivate vegetables for home use, process food such as *chura* (beaten rice) and *ghundruk* (a preserved vegetable), and dry vegetables such as cauliflower and radish. They have almost sole responsibility for child care. For the four months of the peak agricultural season, the women have no leisure time. 'From September through the winter there is some free time but we have to make a special effort to take time off', Damber Kumari said.

Life is not much easier for the men of Lwang. They rise at about 6.30am, then 'some weave *dokos* or mats; some cut fodder; some do nothing', Damber Kumari said. After the morning meal, they work in the fields. Men are responsible for ploughing, preparing the land for planting, making bunds. Some of the work, such as weeding and harvesting is shared. The men bundle and carry the rice straw back to the house. Because rice is the major crop, the responsibility for threshing it falls to the men; women thresh wheat, the minor crop. Some Lwang men have taken up vegetable gardening.

Men have no leisure in the four months when agriculture demands their full attention. After that, the men get some

A Gurung woman's day

Damber Kumari Gurung, who chairs a women's group in the Gurung village of Lwang, in the hills north of Pokhara, says the women of her village prefer a son as the firstborn. Parents in her village used to send their daughters to school for only two to three years. Nowadays, more daughters go to school, and for longer, but their education is never considered as important as their brothers'; if a son goes to a boarding school, for example, the daughter will go to the village school.

time off. 'They are free after about 10.00am. They go to friends' houses to talk. Some only return in the evening. They used to gamble and drink but our women's group banned both', Damber Kumari says. Unlike the Hindu women of many terai communities, Gurung women look after the household finances.

Some 30 years ago, the women of the area formed village groups in order to maintain religious traditions. In 1990, with the encouragement of a local NGO, the Lwang women's group began to broaden its activities. Through literacy classes, the women have learned about sanitation and hygiene, how to maintain trails, build latrines, establish plantations, and so on. The women are now looking at the possibility of establishing a day-care centre for infants. Given the very limited free time available to the women, it seems incredible that they should have achieved so much. In Damber Kumari's words: 'No matter how much we do in the house, nobody notices. But if we work as part of a women's group, what we say and do gets noticed.'

Making salt and butter tea, a traditional Nepali drink

Life in a Mustang village

According to Nima Rita of Putak village, in Lower Mustang, men share rather more of the total workload than their counterparts further south, but they still have less to do than women. People here are ethnically Tibetan, practise a Tibetan-style Buddhism and speak Tibetan as their first language. Men are responsible for ploughing and other physically demanding jobs, such as the maintenance of irrigation systems and the collection and harvesting of dung and fuel wood. Women, in addition to the shared jobs of harvesting, threshing, and fetching manure, are also responsible for planting the main crops, weeding, manuring, grass cutting, cooking, cleaning, food processing, and other domestic tasks, and for the care of children.

Women, like their counterparts in the south, inherit less than men. The first son receives the bulk of the inheritance; the second is usually sent to the monastery and therefore receives nothing. But a daughter will receive less than the third or fourth sons, irrespective of her age. If there is one son and one daughter, the son gets everything and the daughter is given some presents.

Young men and women are allowed to choose their own marriage partners. Sometimes a girl is 'kidnapped'. The parents have three days to find her and ask her if she wants to stay there or come back. If she does not want to stay the boy must give her up. Divorce is easy but not common. The divorcer has usually to pay the cost of the marriage ceremony as a fine. The *mukhya*, the village head, decides on the fine. Remarriage for divorcees is easy, although less easy for a woman. Usually a woman will establish another relationship before embarking on divorce.

Men usually go to the meetings called by the *mukhya*. Failure to attend results in a fine. Women are allowed to attend smaller, less important meetings. Women attend important meetings only if their men are out of town.

Both boys and girls receive primary education; parents failing to send

Washing dishes in a stream, in Kagbeni village.

In addition to religious differences, the hardship of life in the high mountains and the greater interdependency that engenders, may partly explain why mountain women tend to have more power and status. Yet even mountain women are considered by their own society as less important and valuable than men. Sociologists say that this general sentiment makes it easier for society to come to terms with the horrific practice of trafficking of Nepali girls and women for prostitution in Nepali terai towns and Indian cities. This is becoming an increasing problem, as highly-organised gangs, sometimes operating under the protection of local police and politicians, lure away young women from isolated mountain villages, by promising them lucrative jobs in the cities. But instead, they are forced to work in brothels, sometimes as far away as Hong Kong, and inevitably some become infected with sexually-transmitted diseases, including HIV

The Badi community

The Badi are considered by other Nepalis as the lowest of the untouchable castes. Badi men earn a little money from making and selling drums and pipes. They fish, but the catch is usually for home use. Their women sell sex, and their earnings are the main source of income for Badi households. The Badi originally came to West Nepal from India in the fourteenth century. They were travelling entertainers, singing and dancing and relating tales from the Hindu epics. From that time until the end of Rana rule, the Badi were patronised by local rulers and by a few wealthy landlords.

The fall of the Rana regime in the 1950s resulted in loss of authority and income from taxes for the local rulers of West Nepal. They were unable to continue their patronage of the Badi. Badi women then turned to prostitution. In the 1960s, the malaria eradication programme in the terai and the urbanisation that followed provided them with a growing market. At the same time, radio, film and tape players made the traditional Badi occupations of

children to primary school are fined Rs1 per day. But it is the boys who are preferentially sent for higher education. Kausila Sanuwar is a community worker from the terai. She says of her experience with the women of Mustang 'There are great differences compared to our culture. With us the wife is always viewed as inferior to her husband. She must treat him like a Rajah; we have to touch our husbands' feet with our foreheads. But here there is more equality. Without the wife's consent the husband can do nothing.'

singing and dancing redundant and Badi women much more dependent on prostitution.

A recent study of the Badi, who now number some 7,000 in scattered settlements, found that sometimes a client will pay a woman to be exclusively his lover, and the couple may live together for a number of years; in some cases they marry and start families. But such long-term relationships between Badi women and men of high castes rarely last because of opposition from the man's parents and relatives. Unions with men of untouchable castes, however, have been stable and successful.

Another way to earn a living

Despite being shunned by other castes, denied an education either for themselves or their children, being harassed by local authorities and police, there is much positive activity among the Badi communities. Bimala (not her real name), a Badi woman from Kala Khola, is aware of how she and the women of her village have been exploited. She and other women travel to villages where Badi live to spread news about health, hygiene, HIV, and to encourage the women to take up opportunities for study and for learning an alternative means of making a living. In Kala Khola, the Badi have formed *Samaj Sudhar Sewa Sangha*, an organisation that runs adult literacy classes, programmes to raise cultural awareness, an AIDS prevention programme, including door-to-door counselling to raise awareness about HIV and AIDS, and condom distribution, and facilitates alternative income generation by negotiating loans with banks.

An NGO called Self-Awareness for Education (SAFE) is spreading the same message, which seems to have hit home. The Badi women in the red-light area all say the same thing: 'if the client refuses to wear a condom, I tell him to go elsewhere.' The style of prostitution is different among the Badi. Prostitutes live with their mothers and some menfolk; there are no pimps or madams and the community is small.

Tim Malyon/Oxfam

Few girls in Nepal complete primary school, and even fewer go on to secondary education.

SAFE also runs non-formal education classes for adults. A sewing and cutting workshop trains Badi women to produce attractive skirts, bags and other handicrafts in the hope of providing the women with an alternative source of income.

SAFE runs a school for Badi and other underprivileged children and has opened a hostel for Badi boys and girls. 'The idea for the hostel came from the community. They wanted to give their children the chance to study away from the sex, tobacco, alcohol and violence that characterises the red-light area', said Pariyar. 'They want to avoid the girls growing up to be prostitutes and the boys growing up to be thugs.'

The two hostels presently accommodate 22 girls and 18 boys. They are accepted from the age of nine and can stay until they pass their school-leaving certificate. Parents provide clothing and daily food. SAFE's strategy is to teach the children skills, such as furniture-making, hair-cutting, electronics, and so on, so they can return to their communities able to earn a living.

Bimala's point of view

'Traditionally, the *thulabada* ('big men' i.e. the higher status members of society) do not eat food touched by the *Badi*. We were very much shunned. We were treated as the lowest caste even among the backward castes. We were not allowed to go inside [their houses]. We were not even allowed to pass before the cattle sheds lest the animals die, or we touch them and they stop giving milk. We were ignorant. We had no education. Our children were not allowed to study in the *thulabada*'s schools. Our children were taught outside. Still, we survived by singing and dancing.

'Then, when we had beautiful daughters, the *thulabada* used to say "you have to give your daughter to me, how much money do you want?" Our ancestors thought, "the *thulabada* are threatening us and harassing us; we have no land or property; our sisters and daughters have had their virginity taken away by force; so, let's follow this path [prostitution]. At least we will be able to eat." This is how our tradition got spoiled. So, now we do *pesha* (prostitution).

'Now, through our sacrifice we have managed to educate a few of our brothers and they know our pain, our problems and our troubles. They established this (*Samaj Sudhar Sewa Sangha*) organisation. We think that if we can get better employment it will be a lifeline for us, freeing us from *pesha*.

'We are women like any other women. But the community looks at us with different eyes. They see us as the lowest caste, and they see us as prostitutes. It doesn't matter if we wear nice clothes, they just say: "Oh, she does *pesha*". We started hating ourselves and wished, Oh God!, take us from this gutter and put us in a good place.

'Nowadays, a dangerous disease (AIDS) has also come. Because of this disease *dhaal* (condom) is used. We never used to use it, [and so] we had children. Men would keep us for two to four years as "wives", as long as their was colour in our cheeks. Then [they desert so how] to take care of ourselves or raise children?

'The disease is life-taking. Some men say that using *dhaal* is not good, so we have to convince them! We get Rs 50 [per client]. Some men offer Rs 500 [for unprotected sex]. But we convince them, by pleading or whatever, make them happy and let them use *dhaal* even if they do not like it. We say "We want to be saved and you have to be saved too!"'

'Bimala' outside the family home.

Omar Sattaur/Oxfam

Health in the hills

Like all aspects of life in Nepal, the availability of medical care depends on where you live. The comparative wealth of the terai and the ease of transport means that people who live there can more easily get to hospitals and receive specialist health care. But in providing even primary health care for the hill population, government health services have yet to prove their worth.

This is despite an impressive structure for health administration. There are now more than 800 health posts, 12 zonal hospitals, and four regional hospitals. Each health post should be able to perform minor surgery and treat accidents and wounds, and diagnose and treat common ailments. They are supposed to have enough essential drugs and equipment to provide adequate out-patient treatment and to provide home care. Day-to-day work would include advice about preventing illness, and motivating people to vaccinate their children and to use family planning. They should provide pre- and post-natal care and treatment for post-natal gynaecological problems. The staff should consist of a health assistant(HA), two auxiliary health workers (AHWs), two auxiliary nurse midwives (ANMs), one to two maternal and child health workers (MCHWs) and seven to 12 village health workers (VHWs). In addition, each village should be able to draw on the expertise of community health leaders (CHLs), female community health volunteers (CHVs) and traditional birth attendants (TBAs).

The reality is very different. Health posts are inadequately equipped with medicines and poorly managed. Health assistants, people who have completed a two-year Intermediate Science (ISc) qualification in general medicine, are rarely to be found at work. ANMs may be at the health post but their work is usually in the villages. VHWs are supposed to spend 20 days per month in their villages so they are not usually present at the health posts. Apart from the ANMs and volunteers all the rest of the staff are usually male, significant since it is culturally difficult for women to talk to male health workers, particularly about maternal illnesses and gynaecological problems. Thus one of the major functions of the health post in treating maternal and childhood illness is lost.

There are many reasons for these staffing problems. Apart from the VHWs, all other staff are outsiders, posted by the health service to districts they may have no links with. Government policy seems to be to move civil servants every one or two years, so turnover of health assistants is very high. Commitment to the district is therefore not strong and it is common to find that HAs move to terai towns where they can practise privately and thus earn more.

In an attempt to improve primary health care, the government plans to establish 4,000 new sub-health posts, and Primary Health Centres in each of the 205 constituencies. The sub-health posts may prove more effective than the existing health posts, as they are to be staffed by three people: a local VHW, a local married woman as MCHW or Family Planning Worker, and an AHW.

'Geography and ethnicity remain the largest barriers to a really efficient health service' says Dr Mona Bomgaars, who directs the health department at the United Mission to Nepal. The government has done a tremendous job in training TBAs. Nepal is one of the few developing countries that can boast a level of expertise such that, in normal circumstances, its TBAs can provide a hygienic and safe delivery. But there is nothing for the five to 10 per cent of women who have complicated deliveries. One woman per hundred giving birth in Nepal dies because of complications.

District hospitals are not much better equipped than health posts. About 60 per cent of the estimated 1,000 doctors in the country work in the Kathmandu valley. Each district hospital should be staffed by two to three doctors. 'But', says Dr Bomgaars, 'they seldom stay there as there is often no equipment, no technicians, no support staff and they are not adequately trained to meet the needs of the people who would go to a hospital.' She explained that, of the 70 hospitals, only 16 can deal with Caesarean sections; only 14 districts have blood transfusion centres, and only five districts have emergency blood transfusion units.

Traditional healers

Given that health posts may be more than two day's walk away from a village, are often closed, unequipped or unstaffed, not many people bother to visit them. The first choice for treatment are Nepal's estimated 440,000 traditional healers. Healers are well-respected individuals who are recognised as community health leaders. Their methods of treatment are based on a belief that illnesses arise when gods are displeased or when devils are at work. Much of a healer's work may be to do with driving out evil spirits by incantation, blowing mantras, beating drums, and by appeasing gods by offering sacrifices and prayers. Healers are particularly successful in treating mental conditions but can also hinder a person's chances of cure for a physical ailment by delaying other treatment until traditional methods have been tried.

Many development agencies have recognised the importance of healers as community health leaders who can advise and raise awareness of the causes of illness and ways of preventing it, primary health care workers who can cure many common diseases, and diagnose life-threatening conditions and refer them quickly to the health post or hospital. Save the Children UK, for example, has been training healers in primary health care in four districts of Nepal since 1986. The training programme focuses on raising awareness of health services available to the community and promoting their use, encouraging healers to cooperate with health post staff, helping healers to recognise serious treatable diseases and promptly refer people to health posts, teaching about home treatment of diarrhoea, early malnutrition, first aid, communicable diseases, and the need for family planning. The programme also aims to raise awareness among health post staff of the beliefs and practices of healers.

Village health worker.

Ro Cole/Oxfam

Soma Namgyal Lana examines a patient.

Buddhist medicine

Among a group of novice monks chanting Mahayana Buddhist scriptures, Soma Namgyal Lama hopes that there is one who will take his place when he dies. Soma Namgyal is an *amchi*, a practitioner of Tibetan medicine, a dying art in Nepal. Soma Namgyal is worried that he is one of a few remaining Nepali *amchis*.

His medical centre was set up after he cured a group of Japanese tourists who fell ill while trekking in Lower Mustang. They asked him if they could repay him in some way and he asked for a house in which he could treat people. The centre opened four years ago but there are no funds for maintenance, another of the *amchi*'s worries.

There are three *amchis* in the area, and a health post. Gastrointestinal diseases, TB, respiratory illnesses, cardiovascular problems and joint pain are the most common complaints. Since the health post opened, people go there preferentially to treat their wounds. But they opt for traditional medicine first for complaints such as coughs and fevers. The *amchi* thinks both systems are good.

Soma Namgyal studied at Lhasa's foremost Medical College for 13 years. The tradition is that each *amchi* trains his son, but it has broken down. 'Nowadays, no one wants to study. They don't care for mother, father, *dharma*, customs, tradition. They are only interested in themselves', complains Soma Namgyal.

About 500 different substances are used in Tibetan medicine. Some things became difficult to obtain when the border with Tibet closed but Namgyal also believes that the availability of herbs is decreasing. 'There are the same number of species but their quantity is less', he says. The rains of April and May are decreasing. He puts it down to bad collective *karma*. 'People are greedy and sinful. So there is more damage to the environment. Snowfall, and therefore snow melt, is less than before.'

Information for barefoot doctors

'Village health workers are the pillars of primary health care, the first point of contact [with allopathic medicine] for villagers. But they are given six to eight weeks' training and are then forgotten', says Dr Sharad Onta, who heads the Resources Centre for Primary Health Care (RECPHEC) in Kathmandu. His concern about supporting VHWs led RECPHEC to establish two bi-monthly newsletters, Bhalakusari and AIDS, to raise awareness about health issues, prevention of HIV infection and management of AIDS. They are written in simple language and well illustrated so as to attract a general readership, too.

RECPHEC promotes the use of condoms, which are still not widely available in Nepal, certainly not in rural areas. However, a bigger problem is the high rate of condom failure due to incorrect use and poor storage facilities. This means that people have little faith in them. 'There's a lack of awareness about AIDS and how it is spread. Village health workers give injections in the big immunisation programmes, so that's also a big potential risk for spreading AIDS.'

During village immunisation clinics, one health worker may have to immunise 100 babies in a single day. Disposable syringes are not available from the government, and there is no time to boil the needles. RECPHEC are lobbying the government to supply disposable syringes to village health workers. They are also trying to educate the public to counter the widespread belief that injections are needed to treat minor ailments.

RECPHEC held a workshop to identify the training needs of health post staff and discovered that no one ever looked at problems of VHWs. Vaccinations, for example, are not being done simply because of the difficulty of carrying all the equipment — including a vaccine carrier, stove, needles, register and provisions amounting to 10-12 kg — sometimes for days. Yet provision of a simple rucksack would make the task possible. 'As it is no one is going to carry three or four bags that distance. They dump vaccines and report that people have been vaccinated, but that is not the case', says Dr Onta.

Education

Throughout the world, high birth rate is associated with low levels of female literacy. Women who have had some education tend to have fewer children, and their children are healthier on average than children of illiterate mothers. Nepal is caught in a vicious circle; poverty, lack of social security, and high child mortality forces people to have large families. Population pressure means increasing poverty for individuals and the country as a whole. One way of tackling these interlinked problems could be to concentrate more resources on providing education, particularly for women.

Left: Students learning about Nepal's environmental problems.

Below: Child at primary school

Jeremy Hartley/Oxfam

One of the biggest development problems facing Nepal is the low levels of literacy among its people. The adult literacy rate is only 38.7 per cent for men and 12.5 per cent for women. In rural areas the rates are even lower. Trained teachers are reluctant to teach in remote areas. Even if a school is within reach and functioning, children are often needed to work on the land or look after younger siblings, and few of the country's estimated 2.6 million children aged five to nine have the chance to complete primary education. Although enrolment in primary schools has been increasing, and has reached more than 70 per cent, the drop-out rate is very high. Only 27 per cent of those who enter grade I complete the five-year primary course, and only 20 per cent of children go to secondary schools. Primary education is free in Nepal, but fees are charged for secondary schooling.

Saraswati Mahila Club

Saraswati is the Hindu goddess of education. On Saraswati Day, all over Nepal, children have a holiday from school, and go round their village collecting money to buy school books. The Saraswati Club was set up in Bhumrasuwa village, which is a Danuwar community, one of the marginalised ethnic groups. In the clean, neat club office, a hand-written poster on the wall identified the main problem facing the villagers as 'illiteracy', and listed all the activities required in the coming year to organise literacy classes for the village.

Parbati Khadka Danuwar, President of the Club, explained that the aim of the club is to provide education and teach people 'how to live'.

'Women here don't know how to eat, how to dress, they're all illiterate. They live dirtily, they don't wash themselves or their children. They keep food lying around for up to two days before they eat it. They don't have toilets, people just use the fields. We want to change all this. Uneducated women are the main problem, but men too are uneducated here. This is one of the poorest communities in the area. Instead of going to school, the boys have to work on other people's land.

'If they get education, people will understand about health and nutrition, they'll keep their children clean, improve their eating habits. Parents who can read will want to send their children to school, or at least teach them how to read at home.'

So far the club has organised eight different courses, where people can not only learn to read and write, but also about family planning, hygiene, and nutrition.

Parbati admitted that there is a problem once a literacy course ends, as there is no way for people to carry on practising their reading and writing. 'For some of the villagers who come to the literacy class, six months is not enough. They need a whole year.' The club's plans for the future are ambitious. Besides continuing the literacy classes, for which there is steady demand, they want to run income-generation programmes, perhaps enabling people to rear goats or pigs, or providing skills-training, and also set up a scheme for building latrines.

Meeting of the Saraswati Mahila Club.

Ro Cole/Oxfam

Nepal's working children

Helping out with household chores or learning the family business is part of growing up, wherever you happen to be born. But in Nepal, as in many developing countries, children make up a sizeable proportion of the national workforce. Deprived of their chance for education and the time and space to mature at a natural pace, they are forced into earning a living to support themselves or their families or, worse, into bonded labour to pay off a loan.

Nobody knows how many child workers there are in Nepal, but children can be seen working at every kind of job: planting rice, plucking tea, breaking rocks, weaving carpets, domestic service, and prostitution. Indeed, children at work is such a common sight that, for many who live in Nepal, it ceases to provoke comment and becomes 'invisible'.

Nepal signed the UN Convention on the Rights of the Child in 1990 and the new government's Constitution of the same year re-emphasised the prohibition of any form of slavery. Such initiatives have helped to increase the awareness of child rights among the educated, the social activists, and trade unionists. But that awareness has yet to sink into the national consciousness and be transformed into action. It is not uncommon to see domestic child workers employed by well-to-do householders who are aware of child rights and even espouse abolition of child labour; even government-owned tea estates employ children. These contradictions become somewhat easier to understand given the rural Nepali lifestyle — the lifestyle of most of the population — in which children learn to help out from an early age.

Increasing poverty and landlessness, particularly in the middle hills, leave two obvious options open to poor families: to borrow money or to emigrate. Indebtedness to moneylenders, who almost always demand extortionately high interest rates, and the inability to repay loans, often leads to debt bondage of the head of the

Children help with the household chores from an early age. Even quite young girls are given responsibility for looking after younger siblings.

Tim Malyon/Oxfam

household and his family, including his children. Migration from rural to urban areas has increased more than threefold over the past two decades and has given rise to urban squatter settlements whose number and size are growing.

A third, even worse, option for the poorest and most desperate families is the exploitation, as an asset to be bought and sold, of the children's ability to work. Children are now providers of labour, in factories, on other people's land or in other people's houses, taken in lieu of payment of the interest on loans taken out by their parents who are unable to repay. Rural poverty has given rise to a trade in children, operated by brokers who provide child workers to the urban industries, such as carpet and brick factories. Conditions of employment are often appalling.

Child Workers in Nepal (CWIN), a NGO working for the rights of children in Nepal, conducted a survey among carpet factories in the Kathmandu Valley which claimed that all 365 factories visited employed children. Of the 3,322 children interviewed, 65 per cent were between 11 and 14 years and eight per cent were under 10 years old. Ninety-seven per cent were migrants from rural areas and 47 per cent had been brought to the factories by brokers. Two hundred and sixty-five of the children interviewed were bonded labourers, of whom a little more than half knew something of the debt that kept them there.

Temporary or permanent migration, in many cases abroad, of the men of a household is now commonplace in many parts of the country. Remarriage of women deserted by their husbands can save the households, but it is often at the expense of the happiness and security of existing, older children. Family break-ups are common and the casualties are to be seen in the growing number of runaways on the streets of Kathmandu and the major towns of the terai.

Children and the law

The government has drafted a new Labour Act and Children's Act, both of which prohibit the employment of children under 14 years. The Children's Act provides for a potentially effective administration of child welfare, including a national child welfare council overseeing district child welfare boards. At least one child welfare officer is to be appointed in each district, and the Act provides for the establishment of child care centres, shelters and homes for street, abandoned and orphaned children. Existing legislation provides for free education for all at primary level and including the first class in lower secondary school.

The Labour Act is really only applicable to urban industries and not to rural agricultural workers, and their employers, who make up most of the working population. The new Acts are contradictory at times. For example, the Labour Act defines minors (children legally permitted to work) as aged 14 to 18 whereas the Children's Act defines them as aged 14 to 16. The Act also prohibits employment of minors in hazardous occupations but fails to define those occupations.

However inadequate, the legislation has been welcomed by a growing number of organisations dedicated to promoting children's rights. A new networking group called Children At Risk (CAR) was established in 1992 and has attracted some 15 NGOs to attend monthly meetings to discuss child labour, street children, and trafficking.

Growing up on the streets

Ramesh Mahato sleeps in a small park near the roundabout in New Road, a popular shopping street in Kathmandu most famous for its imported consumer goods. He spends his days collecting waste plastics, tin, iron, and copper from rubbish tips. One of the best tips that he works belongs to the Soaltee Oberoi hotel, one of the largest and most expensive hotels in the country. He sells the scrap to junkyard owners who resell it to Indian recycling companies across the border. Ramesh earns a good living, sometimes more than Rs100 per day but, for a 14-year-old without a place to call his home, life is still very insecure.

Ramesh is one of Kathmandu's growing population of street children. He came from Chitwan, in the south of central Nepal, three years ago. He has a younger brother and an older sister. When his father took a second wife, he brought Ramesh and his sister to Kathmandu to work as domestic servants in the home of a well-to-do family. Ramesh says his mother 'ran away' after his father remarried. His father has since settled in India with his new wife; Ramesh's younger brother lives with them.

Ramesh liked the new family he worked for. They treated him well and paid him Rs150 per month. Every year, his father would return to collect Ramesh's wages. He worked for the family for two years until a friend enticed Ramesh to join him for a spree in the city. Once they had grown bored with freedom without money Ramesh went to live with his sister, who had since married and found a job in a garment factory. But after two or three months, Ramesh was forced to leave as there was not enough food to go round. His sister encouraged him to go out to work. Ramesh learned the recycling trade from a friend with whom he teamed up. They would spend the day collecting waste and sell it to a merchant. They split the profits equally.

Ramesh is one of the 500 children who, by 1991, had registered at the CWIN common room. There, Ramesh enjoys a mid-day meal, the company of other children like himself and the chance to use the library and play with the games and toys that the common-room staff make available. If he wants to he can have a shower. He can also receive medical treatment, and see a nurse or counsellor if he needs to. The common room provides children with safe-deposit lockers in which they can deposit their earnings. A savings scheme offers five per cent interest and children are granted emergency loans should they need them.

CWIN opened a transit home for runaways and abandoned or orphaned children. It provides shelter and schooling for children that CWIN has identified as being most in need: the very young, handicapped or ill. The aim is to resettle children within three months, either reuniting them with their families, finding a sponsor or finding them a place in a children's home.

Other organisations in Kathmandu have begun to work with disadvantaged children, running hostels and day centres, providing basic education and training in a variety of skills to enable children to earn a living, and providing counselling to children who have been abused.

Group of street children, Kathmandu. (Keen to be photographed, they stopped playing football and grouped themselves as for an official photo of their favourite team!)

Crispin Zeeman

Giant neighbours

Nepal is a sovereign nation with its own monarch, parliament, language, customs and cultures. Yet it is surrounded on three sides by India, the South Asian giant. Gentle though the giant may be, Nepalis know well the costs of irritating it. On the fourth side, across the high barrier of the Himalayas, lies China. During the cold-war period, Nepal's strategic position meant that China, the USA, and the USSR competed to offer financial assistance. In the 1970s, with the improvement of China's relations with the US, Nepal's importance in the global power game diminished.

With China and India both suspicious of the other's involvement in Nepal's internal affairs, successive Nepali governments have pursued a policy of non-alignment, both globally and regionally, but this has proved a difficult balancing act over the years. In 1989, annoyed that Nepal had bought arms from China and had granted contracts to Chinese construction firms in the terai, and ended preferential treatment for Indian exports, India closed all but two of the 15 border posts after the expiry of the 1978 Trade and Transit Treaty. Within weeks Nepal was deprived of 80 per cent of its usual imports from India and was forced to ration petrol and cooking fuel. India lifted the partial blockade in 1990, and the following year a new Trade and Transit Treaty was signed, guaranteeing quota-free entry of goods, and co-operation on hydroelectric projects and water-sharing.

The two countries have an open border and reciprocal agreement by which Nepalis may work and invest in India with minimal formality and Indians may do the same in Nepal. Uncounted numbers of Nepalis cross the border to look for work, usually as manual labourers, or security guards. Few have enough money to invest in business in India, and even if they did, they would find it hard to compete with Indian traders. On the other hand, the Indian business community is excited about the prospect of a new market in Nepal and Indian business in the country is growing day by day — aided by an exchange rate that gives Indian finished goods the competitive edge. Add to this Indian economic domination Nepal's growing dependence on foreign aid, and the frustration and anti-Indian feeling among Nepalis become readily understandable.

A police raid

Idris Ansari woke up on 27 March 1994 to the sight of several men, armed with staves and pistols, glaring down at him. He felt the touch against his temple of a pistol barrel and heard its owner demand 'Where is Bablu Singh Sardar?' The armed men were Indian police. They were tipped off that an Indian suspected of murder was hiding out in Kathmandu; Ansari's house, in Kathmandu's New Baneswor area, was the second they had stormed into in the course of hunting down their man. They broke open Ansari's cupboards and searched his bedroom while one of the men held Ansari at gunpoint. New Baneswor may as well have been a suburb of New Delhi, the Indian policemen's usual beat. Finally, convinced that Ansari knew nothing about their quarry, the men offered perfunctory apologies and left.

Three days later, Nepal's Home Minister was reported to have sent a note to the Indian Ambassador protesting the intrusion of armed Indian police into the homes of Nepali citizens and suspended the Nepali superintendent of police. A day later, protestors took to the streets and the then opposition Communist Party of Nepal — United Marxist-Leninist (UML) demanded the establishment of an all-party committee to investigate what it referred to as 'a flagrant attempt to flout international law' and to 'encroach upon the territorial integrity of Nepal and national prestige'. Six days after the event, New Delhi's police chief suspended eight policemen involved in the Kathmandu raid and the Indian Prime Minister, P.V. Narasimha Rao, telephoned the Nepali premier to register his regret over the incident.

Both Nepali and Indian citizens and governments were slow to respond, but there is much that is positive in the way the incident was handled. It was reported extensively by newspapers and both governments felt the public pressure to take action. Democracy has brought more transparency to government; people are exercising their right to make their government more accountable to them. At the same time, the slow pace of events triggered off by the New Baneswor raids indicate how novel public demonstration remains to Nepali citizens and how little more India does than pay lip service to Nepali sovereignty.

Advertisement for Indian cigarettes beside a tourist trail in the mountains.

Flight from Bhutan

Nepal's geographical position, squeezed between the two super-powers of India and China, can be an uncomfortable one. But since 1990, a much smaller neighbour, the tiny kingdom of Bhutan, has also been a source of difficulty. In the early 1990s thousands of refugees streamed over the border from Bhutan, across northern India into Nepal. There are still 88,000 Bhutanese refugees in camps in south-eastern Nepal. Some 17,000 more are living with relatives or working in other parts of Nepal or India.

The refugees are ethnic Nepalis — known in Bhutan as Lhotshampas — who speak Nepali and practise Hinduism. Their families had lived in Bhutan for generations, growing rice on small farms in the fertile south of the country. In the 1980s the Royal Government of Bhutan became concerned by the large numbers of ethnic Nepalis in Bhutan. A government census not only showed that the population was much smaller than the 1.2 million hitherto claimed, but that 50 per cent or over were of Nepali origin. This, and political events at the time which brought ethnic Nepali politicians to the fore in neighbouring Sikkim and Darjeeling, may have alarmed Bhutan's rulers, according to Kapil Shrestha, a lecturer in political science at Nepal's Tribhuvan University, and vice-president of the Human Rights Organisation of Nepal. In 1985 the Royal Government of Bhutan enacted a Citizenship Act: Nepalis who could not produce papers proving they were resident in 1958 were declared non-nationals.

The Citizenship Act was followed in 1989 by the policy of *Driglam Namzha* (the 'Bhutanese way of life') which sought to impose Drukpa dress code and other cultural norms on the Lhotshampas. It became illegal to wear anything but Bhutanese national dress in public, and the teaching of Nepali in primary schools was banned. In the same year, a new Marriage Act denied citizenship to spouses of Nepali origin who married after 1958. Children born of such marriages were also deemed aliens. The combined Acts made thousands stateless overnight. Yet another measure which had an impact on the Lhotshampas was the 'green belt policy',

Bhutanese refugees building a classroom at the camp.

Belinda Coote/Oxfam

which sought to transform the rice-growing foothills of southern Bhutan into forest land to maintain ecological balance.

In 1989 a group of ethnic Nepalis formed the People's Forum for Human Rights. The Forum accused the government of infringing basic human rights and petitioned for these rights to be restored. Civil unrest ensued, and was put down by the army and police. According to the Lhotshampas, their public call for a restoration of human rights triggered a wave of government repression and violence, culminating in the mass exodus of the early 1990s. Refugees in the Nepal camps have many stories to tell of harassment, beatings, rape, arson and theft. It was reported that whole villages in southern Bhutan were burned to the ground. The Bhutanese government claims it merely deported illegal immigrants and nipped in the bud the beginnings of a terrorist movement in southern Bhutan.

Life in the camps

Bhim Bahadur Gurung had been head man of his village, in southern Bhutan's Sarbhang District, for 12 years, when, in January 1992, Bhutanese soldiers and police began to harass him and his neighbours. He says he was locked in a cell, tied up and beaten. Two days later he was released, only to find his village burned to the ground. There was no sign of his family. He fled into the forests on the Assam border, and eventually reached the first of the refugee camps to have been set up in Nepal's south-eastern District of Jhapa. There he found his family and thousands of other men, women, and children with similar tales.

In the camps' early days, Oxfam helped to provide drinking water and sanitation. After March 1992, however, its programme became focused on social development. Oxfam worked through the Bhutanese Women's Association, later renamed the Refugee Women's Committee. This counterpart organisation ran non-formal education (NFE) classes for the illiterate, and a supplementary income programme to make the long hours in the camps more productive. Both programmes targeted women, although men also took advantage of the training offered. Another of Oxfam's partners, the Centre for Victims of Torture, has trained refugee women in counselling techniques to help women to cope with the physical and mental abuse they suffered before fleeing Bhutan.

At the height of Oxfam's involvement, each of the eight camps had a bustling Oxfam centre, run by the Refugee Women's Committees, who consulted their fellow-refugees about their priorities. The Oxfam centres were the venue for the NFE classes, training courses in jute weaving and soap-making, and the

While new classrooms are being built, women refugees continue their literacy classes in the open air.

Annemarie Papatheofilou

knitting of jumpers and shawls. These activities were responses to needs which the camp-dwellers had identified. The NFE classes reached nearly 6,000 women. The supplementary income project began with a target of 300 participants but, by early 1993, the number reached had increased to 7,500. UNHCR bought the shawls and sweaters which the women knitted, and these were then distributed to the refugees. The women used the small sums of money they earned to supplement their rations with extra meat, spices, and vegetables.

Due to various constraints, Oxfam wound down much of its programme in late 1995. The Government of Nepal was not happy to allow goods made by the refugees to be sold outside the camps in competition with locally produced goods, making it impossible to sustain the supplementary income programme — there was a limit to the number of shawls and sweaters needed. As a short-term response to problems, however, the programme was regarded as a success by the refugees who took part.

In the current phase of Oxfam's programme, the emphasis is on post-literacy resource centres. Here, the women who learned to read and write on Oxfam-funded NFE courses can read newspapers and public information bulletins, practising their new skills. Without such support, many of them might gradually forget what they have learned. CVICT is also still providing its vital counselling service.

The camps are well kept. Many refugees have established kitchen gardens to supplement their rations. The level of health and well-being is high. Psychological well-being is much more of a problem and is likely to deteriorate as year follows year in the camps. Many refugees complain of having nothing to do. Inevitably there has been some conflict between the camp inhabitants and the local population. The refugees, who receive free food and shelter, provide a large pool of cheap labour because they can afford to work for less than the local people.

Returning to Bhutan is the dream and goal of all the refugees.

Appealing for human rights

Years after they fled from Bhutan, the 88,000 refugees living in the camps in southern Nepal are still stateless and rootless. Unless governments can be prevailed upon to help them, they are likely to remain so. Despite several rounds of bilateral talks between the Bhutan and Nepal governments, there has been no diplomatic progress on the issue. A recent agreement between the two governments to categorise refugees into four separate groups caused controversy because it undermined the refugees' right to return to their homes. India, the major power in the region, has so far refused to involve itself in the search for a solution.

The refugees are represented by two rival groups, the Bhutanese Coalition for Democratic Movement and the Appeal March Coordinating Committee (AMCC). Although they have different strategies, both organisations call for the restoration of human rights in Bhutan and an early repatriation. In its 1995 appeal to His Majesty Jigme Singye Wangchuck, the AMCC declared that, by arbitrarily depriving ethnic Nepalis of their nationality and prohibiting cultural plurality, the Kingdom of Bhutan had contravened the UN Universal Declaration of Human Rights, which it signed up to in 1971.

Various regional and international non-governmental organisations, working on the refugees' behalf, have tried to use the United Nations' human rights machinery to bring about progress towards a resolution of the crisis. To be successful, though, they need one or more national governments to make the plight of the refugees a diplomatic priority

Tourism: who benefits?

Tourism is the country's second largest earner of foreign exchange. According to Government figures, tourism earned the country US$61.09 million in foreign exchange, 20 per cent of total foreign exchange earnings (exports account for a slightly higher percentage). The largest sector are sight-seers — 71 per cent of visitors arriving in 1992 recorded sightseeing as their main reason for going. Business, official work and attending conferences — all urban-based — accounted for a further 16 per cent of arrivals. The great majority of visitors hardly ever venture outside Kathmandu, Pokhara and the major terai towns. A little more than 10 per cent of 1992 arrivals recorded trekking and mountaineering as the main reason for their visit.

Very few tourist dollars reach the villages. Worse still, of the revenue earned from businesses providing services directly to tourists, such as airlines, hotels and travel agencies, much of the profit is leaked away in the cost of necessary imports. One study found that for every Rs100 spent by tourists, Rs62 was spent on imported goods, including items such as air-conditioning units, refrigerators, construction materials and fittings, and vegetables for hotel kitchens. So it seems that much of the foreign exchange earned by the tourism sector never reaches potential beneficiaries, even those in Kathmandu.

A visitor-friendly capital

Kathmandu is described in the guide books as a welcome stop for long-term travellers weary with the difficulties of travel in India and the rest of South Asia. The 'friendliness' of Nepal's people is almost as famed as its sublime mountain landscape. A visit there, even if only to Kathmandu, affords the traveller a glimpse of the country's rich cultural heritage; its unique architecture, the chance to pursue religious studies or simply to rest and enjoy the diverse attractions of the capital.

Thamel, Kathmandu's tourist centre.

Omar Sattaur/Oxfam

Thamel is Kathmandu's tourist centre. There, it is possible to buy goods, clothes and handicrafts from all over South Asia. You can eat Wiener Schnitzel at the Old Vienna Inn, taco and pizza at the Pizza Maya, momo at the Utse Restaurant, and fresh-baked bread from the Pumpernickel Bakery. The 1990 edition of one of the most popular English-language guide book listed 44 good eating places and 40 places to stay in Thamel alone.

At peak season, Thamel can resemble a theme park for the hippie era; unkempt beards and pony-tails, tie-dye frocks and stripy pyjamas never really disappeared from Kathmandu. The tastes of the long-term traveller in food, clothing, and accommodation are well understood and catered for.

The plethora of hotels, guest houses, restaurants, cafes, bars, book shops, boutiques, travel agencies, trekking agencies, and handicrafts shops in Thamel, and the growing sophistication of accommodation and catering along the major tourist routes, suggest that tourism is thriving. In 1962, only 6,172 tourists went to Nepal. Thirty years later that number had increased more than fifty-fold, but just who benefits from tourism is less clear.

Rural environment and the tourist economy

Tourism in the hills and mountains has many potential benefits. It increases demand for vegetables, milk, eggs, and meat, and can thus stimulate agricultural production. Tourists need lodges, restaurants and tea houses, communications, and transport, and buy handicrafts. Tourism provides employment for guides and porters during the agricultural off-season.

However, research into the costs of a British mountaineering expedition showed just how little the rural economy benefits from such expensive visits. About 69 per cent of the total cost was spent outside the country. Of the money spent inside Nepal, nearly half was spent in Kathmandu, including the cost of the climbing permit; and only 14 per cent went on wages to local porters, and just over one per cent on expenses on the journey to the mountain.

Some of the larger tourist agencies claim that high-yield/low-impact tourism is much more beneficial than independent low-budget trekking that Nepal encourages and which is increasing every year. 'Group trekkers leave more money behind in the hills than do individual trekkers'

Tourists come from all over the world to visit Nepal. Here, Austrian tourists meet up with two Indians, who are on a religious pilgrimage to sacred sites.

Opposite page:
Near Ghasa. Spectacular mountain scenery is one of Nepal's major tourist attractions.

says Lisa Choegyal, PR and Marketing Director of one such agency. She says that her company pays camp-site fees, buys as much food as it can locally, carries kerosene, and removes all non-biodegradable rubbish, pays its Sherpas retainers, as well as day-rates when they are on trek, and looks after their medical treatment and health insurance. Other researchers estimate that only five per cent of food required by organised groups of trekkers is purchased locally. In contrast, independent trekkers buy most of their food locally.

But these potential benefits have to be weighed against the negative effects on the environment: increased demand for livestock, fuel wood, and lodges have led to overgrazing and deforestation. Sustainable waste disposal is almost non-existent, and careless disposal of non-biodegradable items is polluting the environment. Finally, increased demand and money supply in rural areas is causing inflation, and thus financial hardship for local populations.

There is certainly a place for a stratagem that prices out environmental degradation. In Upper Mustang, opened to tourists in March 1992, the Government exacts a conservation and development tax on every tourist wishing to visit the area. Upper Mustang is sparsely populated, has hardly any forests, produces very little food, and the ecosystem is extremely fragile. Part of the US$700 charged to each individual for a 10-day permit goes towards conservation and development work with the local communities carried out by the Annapurna Conservation Area Project (ACAP), a local NGO.

Not all tourism in Nepal need be as restrictive as that in Upper Mustang, But letting tourist numbers rise unchecked, with the consequent degradation of the environment and culture, is not the only way of increasing Nepal's earnings from tourism. If visitors could be encouraged to stay longer, and to spend more in Nepal, and if some of the imports required could be replaced by local products, the benefits from tourism could be greater, and be distributed more widely.

Footbridge near Pokhara.

Tim Malyon/Oxfam

Tourism for tomorrow

Ghorepani is a high point for visitors to the Annapurna region, in more ways than one. It is, for many trekkers, a place to relax and enjoy well-earned views of the peaks of Annapurna I, Annapurna South, Hiunchuli, Dhaulagiri I, Tukuche, Nilgiri and others. Well-earned because most will have reached the resort, at 2,775 m, and nearby Pun Hill (3,193 m), after a day's climb from the villages of Tatopani or Birethanti, both some 1,700 m lower.

Ghorepani owes its existence to tourism. The only building to be seen there 25 years ago was a cow shed, according to Dr Chandra Gurung, director of ACAP. The rest, Dr Gurung recalls, was a magnificent ancient rhododendron forest that was almost impenetrable. Word of the spectacular views attracted more and more visitors and there are now about 20 lodges at Ghorepani, all built from the forests that were cleared. The lodge-keepers vied with one another to provide the most luxurious service. Hot showers, camp fires, and menus so varied as to tickle the taste buds of anyone from Mexico to Madras made huge demands on the forests for fuel wood. Researchers in 1987 estimated that some lodges were burning up to 330 kg of wood per day to satisfy the demands of tourists for food and hot water — enough to meet the needs of a local six-member household for a month or more.

Due to the efforts of NGOs like ACAP, tourism in Ghorepani is much more fuel-efficient today. A visitor centre educates trekkers about the environmental issues and how to enjoy Nepal without harming it. Most of the lodge kitchens now have a back boiler — a galvanised iron drum half sunk into the traditional mud-walled cooking stoves. At the same time as the heat from the burning wood cooks food or heats kettles, it also heats water pipes that lead to the drum. The common sitting rooms and dining areas in the lodges are heated by fuel-efficient space heaters.

Fuel-efficient space-heater in a tourist lodge.

People-friendly conservation

But ACAP's work is not only concerned with fuel-efficient technology. The organisation, a project of the King Mahendra Trust for Nature Conservation, was established in 1986 to find ways of development which would not damage natural and cultural integrity. 'For 15 years, the Trust had a 'preserve' mentality, with fencing and army guards to preserve and protect the resource from encroachers.' In 1985, 75 per cent of the country's budget for its (then) seven national parks was spent on paying the army to keep people out. 'There was an urgent need for an approach that addressed the development needs of the local inhabitants as well as the needs of tourists and conservationists,' Dr Gurung explains. The focus area was the Annapurna region, which attracts 64 per cent of all tourists trekking in Nepal.

There are many reasons for its popularity. The area is home to people of a wide range of ethnicities including Manangi, Bhotia, Magar, Thakali, Gurung, Tamang as well as the Hindu castes. The visitor can not only appreciate the changing landscape, agricultural systems, and architecture but also the various lifestyles and cultures of the people who live there. In the more remote parts of the region can be found musk deer, red panda, snow leopard, and blue sheep. Visitors to the area must pay a conservation fee of Rs 650 per week, which is channelled into conservation and development activities in the area, such as forest conservation, tourist awareness programmes, and community development projects.

Dr Gurung stresses the need to first 'win the hearts of the people' in order to achieve real participation in decisions on priorities for development, and designing and implementing projects. But he is also realistic about the time scale; winning trust and raising awareness about natural and cultural conservation takes a long time. The area also attracts the interest of visiting philanthropists. A school, drinking water scheme, and a medical post have already been established by outside donors. Many lodge owners are critical of ACAP. They want a microhydro scheme to bring electricity to the village, and claim that ACAP is not working fast enough. They know that if they cannot get ACAP to do things their way, and at their pace, they will be able to find alternative sources of funding.

Educating the visitors

Environmentally conscious individuals and groups in Nepal are trying to educate tourists and communities about ways of making tourism sustainable. ACAP has devised a minimum impact code for tourists which is delivered with trekking permits to the Annapurna area. Another group, called Kathmandu Environmental Education Project (KEEP), offers advice on cultural and environmental sensitivity to tourists from their office in Thamel, Kathmandu's main tourist area. KEEP also holds training workshops for guides and cooks on fuel-efficient cooking on trek, educating tourists about disposing of human waste and non-biodegradable items and respecting the culture. Sagarmatha National Park has published *Trekking Gently in the Himalaya*, with assistance from the World Wide Fund for Nature, which is full of useful tips for trekkers. The main points from all of these codes are listed below.

- **Save wood.** Be self-sufficient in fuel. Use kerosene and wear warm clothes. Do not make open fires and do not ask for hot showers unless the lodge has a back boiler or uses kerosene. Choose to stay at lodges that have energy-saving devices such as back boilers, space heaters and fuel-efficient stoves. Avoid ordering six different kinds of Western food at different times; if your group orders local food, all at the same time, it will help to save fuel. Take water-purifying tablets or filters with you rather than asking for boiled water, unless you stay at lodges with back boilers.

- **Do not pollute.** Burn all dry paper, if possible in an established fire pit. Bury biodegradable items. Pack out non-biodegradable items such as bottles, plastics and batteries, or deposit them in rubbish pits if available. Use toilets when available. If none exist, ensure that you are at least 20 metres away from a water source and bury your waste. Do not shampoo in streams or hot springs and try to use biodegradable shampoos and soaps. Supervise trekking staff to make sure they cover toilet pits and dispose properly of wastes.

- **Camp conservatively.** Choose established campsites whenever possible, even if it means sharing a site with another group. Avoid trenching around tents; if the site is sloping and on high ground, a plastic sheet under the tent should prevent seepage of rain.

- **Tread carefully.** Do not walk through planted fields and be careful not to destroy bunds. Close all gates after you and repair anything you damage, such as dry stone walls or water conduits. Steer clear of water buffalo, yaks and donkeys on the trail in case they bolt. Stick to the main trail. Steeper trails encourage erosion. Do not make new trails across meadows and do not walk through shrubs.

- **Be a guest.** Do not damage, disturb or remove any plants, animals, animal products or religious artefacts. Respect local customs in your dress and behaviour. Women should not wear shorts or revealing blouses and men should always wear a shirt. Avoid outward displays of physical affection. Dress decently when visiting monasteries and remove your shoes. Do not offer half-eaten food to people. Never point your finger, feet or step over someone. Give and receive with both hands. Do not dip into food to be eaten by others. Ask permission to take photographs and respect people's right to privacy. Do not encourage begging by giving to beggars. Do not barter for food and lodging — many communities have established lodge management committees that set standard rates. Encourage young Nepalis to be proud of their culture.

- **Remember the ACAP motto.** Nepal is here to change you, not for you to change Nepal.

Whose environmental problem?

The litter left behind by mountaineering and trekking expeditions has given the Everest base camp a new nickname of the world's highest rubbish tip. The discovery led to worldwide publicity and concern which spawned several local and international clean-up campaigns. The sullied Everest became an environmental issue that evoked shame and anger. But, as Lhakpa Norbu Sherpa, former warden of Sagarmatha and Rara national parks, points out: 'To local residents, the question of litter on the High Himal is not a big issue because they have no business to go up there unless paid to do so by a foreign expedition. It is an out-of-sight, out-of-mind matter for most... From the perspective of the local inhabitants of the Khumbu, the declining agricultural and pastoral productivity, inflation, shrinking forest reserves and rapid cultural erosion are of equal concern, if not greater.'

Clearly, perceptions of what constitutes an environmental problem vary. For example, the inhabitants of the major towns in the terai and the Kathmandu Valley are justifiably disturbed by atmospheric pollution caused by motor vehicles — infections of the upper respiratory tract are now accepted as the price to pay for living in the capital, as is the fact that the Himalayan snow peaks are now much less frequently visible from Kathmandu. But atmospheric pollution is not something much thought about in the middle hills and high mountain, where more than half the population of the country live.

In the mid-1970s, Nepali farmers were being blamed for exporting, free of charge, Nepali soil to the extent that new islands were being formed in the Bay of Bengal (*char*s). Mismanagement in the middle hills was supposed to have increased flooding downstream. Although it is true that loss of tree cover exposes the soil to rain and wind, thereby increasing its erosion, particularly from steep slopes, those losses have to be put in perspective. Closer analysis suggests that, although

Nepal is largely dependent on wood for most of its energy needs.

Jeremy Hartley/Oxfam

deforestation affects the amount of local erosion and run off, it contributes very little to major flooding elsewhere. Soil erosion and sedimentation is higher from degraded and overgrazed forests, but it will always have been high in an active mountain-forming area such as the Himalaya.

This is not to deny the negative impacts of deforestation, however, which has greatly contributed to poverty and emigration. Nepalis in town and country rely on wood for fuel. In rural Nepal, 98 per cent of energy consumed is derived from wood; the figure is 83 per cent for urban areas. However, the perceptions of outsiders about the country's ecological crisis was very different from those of its inhabitants. People knew very well the limits of their ecosystems and had evolved ways of coping which, as is often the case, crumbled under the power of external forces (in this case, legislation which robbed them of ownership of forest resources).

Today, many forests are in better shape. Landowners have responded to the fuel crisis by planting more trees on their lands, and planting in private forests has also increased. Although deforestation is still a problem in pockets of the terai, most of the forest land in the hills that could have been converted to crop land has been cleared for that purpose, and so loss and gain of forest cover has stabilised. Afforestation projects are gradually increasing tree cover in the hills.

The decreasing fertility of the soil is also of great concern. Farmers traditionally fertilise their land with green manures and livestock dung. Fertilisers are available and used mostly in the terai, although hill farmers whose lands are close to road heads have access and, if funds permit, will purchase fertilisers.

Springs, streams and rivers and wells provide water for most of the rural population. Lack of sanitation often leads to contamination of the water supply, and gastrointestinal infections are common. The studies of water quality that have been carried out in the Kathmandu Valley, and major towns show that, despite chlorination, the piped supplies are rarely safe. Water pipes often run parallel to sewage pipes; low pressure and their state of disrepair leads to contamination. Industries, growing in the capital and towns of the terai, use rivers as tips for untreated wastes. This has led to such a deterioration of water quality in rivers, Kathmandu's Bagmati, for example, that they are no longer able to support aquatic life at certain stretches. Once a destination for ritual bathing, pilgrims now think twice about dipping into the Bagmati at Kathmandu.

Silt washed from eroded hillsides being deposited in the bend of a river

Environmental care, from the ground up

A group of schoolchildren stand in a circle. In the centre, a group leader holds a ball of string. This facilitator is playing the role of the Sun. The Sun's rays support all plant life, played by another child in the ring. The facilitator holds the end of the string and passes the ball on to the 'plant child'. Cows eat plants, so the 'plant child' grasps the string and passes the rest on to child playing the role of the cow. And so the ball is passed from one child to the other, forming a web, a visual representation of the web of life, the interdependencies between living organisms in an ecosystem. What happens if farmers start to use pesticides? Insects living on the plants would die so 'insect child' lets go of the string; 'frog child', which eats insects, lets go too; 'snake child', which eats frogs, similarly, lets go. The web begins to sag and eventually disintegrates.

This game is one of the 600 or so activities that the volunteers of ECCA have invented or collected from around the world in order to teach Nepali schoolchildren about their environment. ECCA stands for Environmental Camps for Conservation Awareness, five-day training camps in environmental awareness and intervention for school children. ECCA first identifies interested members of a local group — perhaps simply a sports club — with whom to work. ECCA trainers then train some members of the group in conservation issues and how to facilitate a camp. The trainers then pass on this information during the five-day camps to schoolchildren. Those children then take the message and expertise home to their parents and, thus, the rest of the community. 'Very often the problem exists, the solution exists but somewhere, the two are not linked', says Anil Chitrakar, a founder-member of ECCA.

Almost no written material is used in the camps. Games, experiments, practical training and fun take the place of books.

Gathering fuel wood,

Jeremy Hartley/Oxfam

Jeremy Hartley/Oxfam

During the camp, 10 boys and 10 girls, chosen to represent the ethnic and caste diversity of the village, go on a nature hike around their village, designed to make them ask questions about the sustainability of natural resources. Children also learn about arts and craft, culture, technology, health and sanitation and so on.

After the camps, parents are invited to a workshop in which they and their children discuss what they can do to solve the major environmental problems identified by the children. It may be lack of fuel wood, or river pollution. For Saraswoti Khanal of Bal Sundar School, in Nayapati near Kathmandu, the camp was an unforgettable experience. She had learned how to make a smokeless stove and, with the help of counsellors, installed one in her own home after the camp. Her parents were delighted. After camps in the Sheopuri watershed area, the demand for smokeless stoves shot up dramatically, despite the existence for more than one year of a project to promote their use.

'There have been schools where, following a camp, children have demonstrated for a toilet to be installed; others where children have written to the Prime Minister on environmental problems', said Anil Chitrakar. In 1986, when ECCA was formed, six camps were held and the number has been increasing every year. The NGO now covers 32 out of Nepal's 75 districts.

Community forestry comes of age

Local people know their forests and know what they want from them. Nepal is one of the few developing countries to have reflected this in legislation. The Forest Act 1994 empowers District Forest Officers (DFOs) to hand over ownership of national forest to users' groups as community forests. DFOs grant forest users' groups (FUGs) certificates of entitlement once they are satisfied with the groups' operational plans, which outline how the forests are to be managed and how their products are to be sold and distributed.

The community forest legislation came just in time. Successive waves of occupation of the terai, from the nineteenth century to the present day, have led to the destruction of large tracts of what was once almost impenetrable forest, and the degradation of the remaining forests. Pressure from a growing population in the middle hills has led to the clearance of forests for agriculture; a process that is almost complete today.

The largest wave of deforestation in the hills occurred after 1957, when, in a well-meaning but ill-fated move, the government nationalised the forests. Communities lost their sense of ownership, and older systems of community management of forest resources crumbled. A decade or more of widespread deforestation ensued, despite the Government's deployment of armed soldiers to guard the forests. Indeed, it was said that the health of the forests was a good indicator of the health of the government: when the government was weak, the forests were plundered. The landscape of Nepal has profoundly changed. More than 80 percent of the land below 4,000 metres was once forested, but now only 19 per cent of the country remains under tree cover. In the 1970s and 1980s, Nepal was widely reported to be on the brink of ecological disaster.

However, reforestation programmes in the 1970s are beginning to show their effects in certain areas, although the new forests have been established on grazing and shrub land and the species planted are often not as useful as indigenous species. Scarcity of fuel wood, fodder and timber in the middle hills has stimulated more planting of useful trees on private lands.

The handing over of government forests to FUGs is helping to consolidate a stabilisation of forest cover in the middle hills. In the eastern hills, in which the British Overseas Development Administration (ODA) has been supporting community forestry since 1979, FUGs are well established and many have succeeded in successfully rejuvenating community forests. In the words of one woman, Maling Phang Rai, a member of Pakha FUG in Dhankuta municipality: 'Before we formed the group

Opposite page:
Parlepani tree nursery. These seedlings will be used in reforestation schemes, and will eventually produce timber useful for housebuilding.

Hills near Chautara. Reforestation is beginning to show results in some areas.

the forest guards used to steal the products. There was never any good grass or good wood. We who depended on the forest were always in the position of thieves. Now all this is changed. We can cut when we want.'

Maling Phang's words reveal the radical changes that have taken place since ownership of the forest passed into the hands of her community. The FUG's operational plan has effectively protected the forest, managed its resources to benefit the whole community, and imposed fines on those who disobey its regulations: erstwhile 'thieves' have become responsible managers. Her FUG has taken advantage of government subsidies on vegetable seeds and use patches of forest land to cultivate vegetables for sale.

A change has also taken place in the attitude of forest officials. A joint project run by the Nepal-UK Community Forestry Project and the District Forest Office (DFO) has been set up to run workshops for Rangers, Assistant Rangers and Forest Guards, which emphasise the importance of self-government of forests and the valuable role that forestry staff can play in stimulating the formation of FUGs and supporting them when established. The training lasts three weeks, and half the time is spent in a village, to facilitate the formation of a FUG and help to prepare the operational plan.

While members of FUGs in general fully understand the community forest legislation and their joint responsibilities once they assume ownership, the individual members' responsibilities and rights to modify operational plans to suit their needs is less clear. This ignorance of rights is often seen in female FUG members even though women, rather than men, are responsible for collecting fuel wood and fodder and therefore have much more to do with the day-to-day management of forests.

For example, Damber Bishwokarma, as a single mother of three children, found the responsibilities of membership of her local FUG hard to cope with. Her husband left to work in Saudi Arabia, and Damber Bishwokarma tries to survive on her tiny plot of land and by working on other people's fields. She had to participate in the community planting of seedlings in the forest, as laid down in the FUG's operational plan, or pay a fine of Rs50. Each time, she had to leave her children at home, She had to cook a meal for them when she returned in the evening. Since formation of FUG, four months ago, no one has been allowed to collect wood from the forest. Since grass and fuel wood from her own land is insufficient, Damber Bishwokarma has to spend a long time gathering it from more distant areas. But Damber Bishwokarma has not felt able to explain her difficulties at the FUG meetings. 'Sometimes I attend the meetings. After one of them, I spoke to the secretary and other committee members about the fact that I have no free labour. But they just said that I would have to go to do the community work anyway.'

Other women are more outspoken: 'Before, I used to spend about two hours collecting good firewood. Now I have spend five hours and it is not very good wood. It is us women who have to collect the wood, not the men.'

But they realise the importance of protecting the forest. 'So far, we haven't complained because, if we do, where would we get wood in the future? The forest is ours. If they allow us to cut wood it will be completely finished.' Now the women burn maize husks, stubble and some fodder species which are all hard to cook with and much faster burning. Not only is their fuel of lower quality but it takes them much longer to collect.

It is all too common for the needs of women to be ignored, even though they are members of their FUGs. The women felt that their personal hardship did not justify jeopardising the health of the forests and therefore the greater good of their communities.

The rules have been made without their participation, despite the project's recognition of the need, during the formation of FUGs, to set up sub-groups that represent weak, disadvantaged or special-interest groups, such as women, low-caste groups or fuel-wood vendors. These sub-groups are then supposed to raise their needs before the village agrees an operational plan. According to the team leader of the project, a separate strategy to ensure the participation of poor women in the running of FUGs is being developed, in a fresh attempt to create a truly empowering environment for all forest users.

Ring-barking on a hardwood tree preparatory to felling.

People power

Tim Malyon/Oxfam

The birth of lobbying and human rights organisations illustrate the new freedoms that Nepali citizens enjoy since the demise of the Panchayat system. Such groups are becoming increasingly articulate and armed with the skills required to lobby with government and multilateral institutions.

When the World Bank decided to abandon the long-planned and controversial Arun III hydroelectric power project, it is likely that the decision was to some extent influenced by opposition from Nepali pressure groups such as the Alliance for Energy. Some countries, such as Germany and the USA, which had originally pledged funds to the World Bank for Arun III, had become more cautious about the project, largely because of pressure from environmental groups in their countries. Such large-scale projects create enormous disruption, displacing many thousands of communities, and their long-term performance is less cost-effective than was once thought. The World Bank is now planning to help Nepal to develop several smaller hydroelectric schemes, in place of Arun III.

In smaller ways, a new sense of freedom is being felt and expressed even in rural Nepal. The increased transparency of the processes of government, the rapid growth of print media, the increasing reach of non-formal education initiatives are all helping to increase the confidence of villagers in their own ability to shape their futures.

The Chelibeti Club, near the inner-terai district town of Gaighat, is a small example of this positive trend. Women from Bhujal, Magar and Rai communities from a village called Baraghare and a squatter settlement of landless people on the banks of the river below Baraghare formed this women's group in 1991. All are considered low-caste in the area. They run literacy classes and a discussion group, network with other NGOs in the area, run a savings scheme and an income generation project involving goat rearing. According to Tara Kumari Rai, president of the Club in 1994, 'Although the village is near the town, the women here don't know anything about education. But after we ran the non-formal education class, they understood that education is important. Now they are aware, and that's the main benefit. Now we are a group, not just individuals, we feel we can achieve something.'

One thing they achieved, against tremendous odds, was to build a road from their village to the district town of Udaipur. They wanted a road because the old path was long and circuitous, between fields along bunds which would become increasingly obscured as the crops matured. The club members also thought that easier access would raise the price of their land and attract better-off people to settle in their village. The land belongs to the government but, throughout Panchayat times, was farmed by a powerful land-owning family. During the first phase of building the road, there were 300-400 volunteers digging. They made half of the 3-km road three times only to have it destroyed during the night by members of the family who were farming the land and therefore opposed to the road. Each time the volunteers rebuilt the road.

Tara Kumari Rai recalls, 'all the people helping us to dig were very poor and had no money for food, but we didn't have food to give them. My second child was only 25 days old. I had to leave the baby with my mother-in-law, she fed the baby with cows' milk. Sometimes we asked ourselves, "why are we doing this?"'

The clubs opponent's have already taken the members to court and lost. 'We thought, why are we bothering, it's not as if the road is just for out benefit! We had no time to eat. We were so tired, and then we had to go to court as well,' Tara Kumari Rai recalls. Yet the club members struggle on to fight for what they know is their right.

This struggle would probably never have happened in the old days. But old norms are constantly challenged today. Even caste divisions are beginning to break down as more and more villagers begin to see the value in standing together to improve their lives. However limited the power of democracy nationally, it is helping to empower people locally.

Opposite page: Small-scale hydroelectric scheme in the middle hills, near Tatopani. This type of development could greatly benefit the country's economy and improve the lives of Nepalis.

Tulashi Pandua joined the Chelibeti club to learn to read and write. With her new-found confidence, she quickly got involved in other activities, including goat-rearing. The club provided her with some breeding goats, and when they produce kids which she can sell, she will pay back to the club the value of her goats.

Annemarie Papatheofilou

Facts and figures

Land area: 137,000 square kilometres

Population: 20.3 million (1992)

Population growth rate: 2.6% p.a. (population will double by 2019 if present rate of growth continues)

GNP per capita: 170 US$

Main exports: carpets, ready-made garments, rice, timber

Main imports: fuel, chemicals, manufactured goods, fertiliser

Daily calorie intake: 1,957 per capita

Adult literacy: 25.6% (male 38.7%, female 12.5%)

Life expectancy: 53.5 years (male 54, female 53)

Maternal mortality rate: 830 per 100,000 live births (1980-92)

Infant mortality rate: 99 per 1000 live births

Under-five mortality rate: 128 per 1000 live births

Children under five who are underweight: 51% (1990)

1 doctor for every 16,667 people.

(Sources: UNDP and Economist Inteligence Unit)

Oxfam in Nepal

Oxfam has been funding projects in Nepal since the 1960s. At first, support was given to organisations working at national level on improving the country's health care capacity: the provision of hospital equipment, work with sufferers from Hanson's disease and TB, and long-term support to rural community health services.

The level of Oxfam funding increased substantially in the 1980s as contacts were made with counterpart Nepali organisations who could work directly with disadvantaged groups such as destitute women, child labourers, and low-caste groups. With democratisation in 1990 it became easier for Nepali NGOs to register, and Oxfam supported their work in rural communities on income generation, adult literacy, and water and sanitation.

Throughout the years, Oxfam has also provided help to communities devastated by disaster. In 1989 and 1991 emergency assistance was provided to a district in which houses had suffered severe damage by earthquake and fire. Again, in 1993 Oxfam responded when crops and houses in some parts of the country were destroyed by flooding.

When southern Bhutanese fled from their country and sought refuge in Nepal, Oxfam joined with UNHCR and other international agencies to provide assistance in the refugee camps in eastern Nepal. Programmes for refugee women focused on a variety of income-generating projects and an adult literacy programme, which has now incorporated discussion groups where refugees can share their problems and concerns.

The Oxfam Bridge programme works closely with small-scale crafts producers, helping them to develop successful marketing strategies and to improve their productivity. The aim is to ensure that the producers, usually poor women living in rural areas, are paid fairly for their work. Some of their products are sold through Oxfam shops in the UK and the Oxfam mail-order catalogue, as well as in craft shops for tourists visiting Kathmandu.

Oxfam believes that its most important contribution is in strengthening the capacity of local organisations who are working side by side with poor people in their efforts to develop sustainable livelihoods and become full participants in their society, with the right to benefit from the resources of their country and full recognition of their basic rights as citizens. To this end, Oxfm works in close partnership with Nepali NGOs who carry forward innovative projects in adult literacy, sustainable agriculture, community development, and income generation, among other activities.

Members of an Oxfam-supported women's group

Belinda Coote/Oxfam

Further reading

Agarwal B, *A Field of One's Own: Gender and Land Rights in South Asia*, Cambridge University Press, 1995.

Ghimire K, *Forest or Farm? The Politics of Poverty and Land Hunger in Nepal*, Oxford University Press, 1992.

Gray J N, *The Householder's World: Purity, Power, and Dominance in a Nepali Village*, OUP, 1995.

Hisham M A et al, *Whose Trees? A People's View of Forestry Aid*, Panos Publications, 1991.

Human Rights Watch, *Rape for Profit: Trafficking of Nepali Girls and Women to India's Brothels*, HRW, New York, 1995.

Hutt M, *Nepal: A Guide to the Art and Architecture of the Kathmandu Valley*, Kiscadale, 1994.

Gellner D N and Quigley D, *Contested Hierarchies*, Clarendon Press, 1995.

Salkeld A, *People in High Places*, Cape, 1991.

Sattaur O, *Child Labour in Nepal*, Anti-Slavery International, 1993.

Soussan J et al, *The Social Dynamics of Deforestation*, Parthenon, New York, 1995.

World Bank/UNDP, *Nepal: Poverty and Incomes*, World Bank, Washington, 1991.

Evening, Kathmandu.